Forced to Choose

FORCED TO CHOOSE

France, the Atlantic Alliance,
and NATO—Then and Now

Charles G. Cogan

PRAEGER

Westport, Connecticut
London

FORCED TO CHOOSE

France, the Atlantic Alliance,
and NATO—Then and Now

Charles G. Cogan

Westport, Connecticut
London

Library of Congress Cataloging-in-Publication Data

Cogan, Charles.
   Forced to choose : France, the Atlantic Alliance, and NATO—then and now /
Charles G. Cogan.
     p.   cm.
   Includes bibliographical references and index.
   ISBN 0–275–95704–7 (alk. paper)
    1. France—Military policy. 2. France—Foreign relations.
3. North Atlantic Treaty Organization. 4. France—Politics and
government—1945–1958. I. Title.
UA700.C593 1997
355'.033044—dc21   96–45330

British Library Cataloguing in Publication Data is available.

Library of Congress Catalog Card Number: 96–45330
ISBN: 0–275–95704–7

First published in 1997

Praeger Publishers, 88 Post Road West, Westport, CT 06881
An imprint of Greenwood Publishing Group, Inc.

Printed in the United States of America

The paper used in this book complies with the
Permanent Paper Standard issued by the National
Information Standards Organization (Z39.48–1984).

10 9 8 7 6 5 4 3 2 1

Copyright Acknowledgments

The author and publisher gratefully acknowledge permission to reprint the following material:

Selections from Vincent Auriol, *Journal du septennat, 1947–1954*, vol. 1 (Paris: Armand
Colin, 1974). Reprinted by permission of the publisher.

Selections from Maurice Vaïsse, Pierre Mélandri, and Frédéric Bozo, eds., *La France et
l'OTAN, 1949–1996* (Brussels: Éditions Complexe, 1996). Reprinted by permission of the
publisher.

Contents

Introduction

Since the theme of this study is "From the Victory to NATO," covering the period 1945 to early 1952 in the France-NATO relationship, it should be explained what is meant by the "Victory." In May 1945, in the words of François Furet, "France came out of the war like a wounded nation, led by its healer."[1] Furet points out the contrast between November 11, 1918, and May 8, 1945, citing the description of Raymond Aron:

November 1918. . . . What was Paris on the day of the armistice, on the day after the armistice, no one can imagine. One has to have seen it. People were embracing in the streets. Everyone: the bourgeois, the laborers, the office workers, the youth, the old people; it was a sort of mass madness, but it was a joyful madness. . . . On the contrary in the month of May 1945, Paris was mortally sad, the Paris that I saw. I remember a conversation I had with Jules Roy on that day. He was struck, as was I, by this sadness, this absence of hope. It was the victory of the Allies more than it was that of France. [It was] nothing at all like the transports of enthusiasm of the days of November 1918.[2]

Even today, as Stanley Hoffmann has put it, "It is the Liberation [of Paris in August 1944] that [the French] celebrate, rather than the victory of May 1945."[3] The Liberation of Paris was the instant that the French people discovered their faraway savior, General de Gaulle, whose force of personality had made it appear for one ephemeral moment that his Free French forces alone had liberated the city. The victory of May 1945, on the other hand, referred the French back to the origins of the war and the debacle of 1940, leaving—in the formula of Professor Hoffmann—two characteristics in the collective memory: catastrophe and humiliation.

Thus, in the words of Robert Frank, "that which is sadly memorable is not easily commemorable."[4]

November 1918 was an altogether different event. In the words of a certain Captain de Gaulle, France had returned, after a century, to having "[a] military force, the first in the world today."[5] France was at the zenith of its power at that moment, and the relief and exhilaration at the end of the war and the recovery of the "lost provinces" of Alsace and Lorraine were boundless.

But France was at a false zenith in 1918: It emerged from the war with the world's most powerful army, but it was exhausted as a nation. It had borne the brunt of the war on the western front on the Allied side. Its war dead, 2,385,000, were half again those of Great Britain and twelve times those of the United States.[6]

At a 1990 conference on Charles de Gaulle in New York, Henry Kissinger observed that "nothing is more poignant than the French effort of the 1920's and 1930's to construct the Maginot Line, which was done at a moment when the German army was limited to 100,000 men, when the Rhineland was demilitarized, and when the French army was the largest in Europe."[7]

And yet, as Kissinger also stated on the same occasion, "France understood clearly that its world had ended in 1918 and that it could never withstand Germany alone." The demographic factor was palpable: Between 1935 and 1939, according to Stephen Schuker, the number of French youths becoming of draft age (what the French call a "classe") was only half of what it had been in previous years, due to the casualties of World War I. The corresponding number of youths coming of draft age in Germany in the same period was twice that of France. The French population at the time amounted to 39 million. Germany's was half again as much.[8]

Still, as Hoffmann pointed out, when the moment of truth came on May 10, 1940, the attacking Germans did not have more men, and did not have more tanks, than their opponents on the western side of the front. It is not the purpose of this study to go into the causes of the French defeat in 1940, which has been one of the great subjects of twentieth century historiography. But it remains one of the great mysteries of the interwar period that France, with not much more than the same percentage of human losses in World War I as Germany, was physically and morally exhausted by the conflict, while Germany, by the middle of the 1930s, manifestly was not. The fact that France had emerged victorious from World War I offers only a partial explanation.

In World War II, the numbers of French killed were much less (120,000 in the Battle of France, 600,000 for the entire war, including civilians), but it had endured more than four years of occupation. By the time the occupation ended, France, which had been invaded three times in the span of seventy years (1870–1940), saw itself as the principal victim of the rise of Germany. Therefore France, considerably more than her Anglo-American allies, had a primordial interest in keeping her turbulent neighbor weak. So, thought the members of the new French Provisional Government, did Soviet Russia.

At the end of the Second World War, as at the end of the First World War, France had designs on German territories and resources that her two Western allies did not share. Charles de Gaulle's call of "Long Live Rhineland France"[9] did not represent merely the general's tendency toward aggressive overstatement. It was an expression of the ancient French desire for a "natural frontier" on the east of France at the Rhine such as existed on its other borders. Soviet Russia, with an equal interest in keeping Germany down, was, in Gaullist planning, possibly if not likely to be a supporter of France's aims. It was a misreading that would die slowly and hard.

It should also be kept in mind that of all the great nations of Europe, France was the only one that was conquered by Germany during the Second World War—the term "great nation" being understood to refer to the historical notion of the traditional European concert of nations: Great Britain, France, Russia, Prussia, and Austria-Hungary. Because France was in this pre-eminent category in history, the rapid collapse of 1940 was felt all the more keenly; the shock was all the more intense.

This having been said, being historically one of the great nations of Europe also meant that France would be expected to have a say as to the kind of peace that would be established after the fighting was over. The corollary of this was that France, being the biggest of the countries that had succumbed to the Germans and had been occupied by them, was in the best position in the West to argue forcibly that the rapid recovery of the former enemy was unacceptable.

Though peace had arrived in May 1945, France's hardships and mental anguish would continue for more than a decade. As Furet characterized it, France in the twentieth century had "a bad experience with both victory and defeat."[10] France had been unable to secure its victory of 1918, it had been crushed in 1940, and in 1945 it was in an extraordinarily unique situation: "Neither victorious nor defeated, or rather, both victorious and defeated." It had gone down to defeat in 1940 and its role in the triumph of 1945 had been essentially peripheral.[11]

By managing to become a permanent member of the United Nations Security Council and a part of the four-power governing body over Germany, France had recovered the appearance of its rank but not, however, the reality of its influence.[12] It would take years before France would emerge from its weakness and its sense of shame. This would eventually be accomplished at the end of the 1950s through Charles de Gaulle, cast aside by the political parties shortly after World War II but whose image had remained incorruptible ever since his call to continue the war on June 18, 1940.

During the entire period that stretched from the Victory to the creation of the North Atlantic Treaty Organization, the image and the position of France was one of a weak state. Its status as a major power was recognized, but only as virtual. It was in a state of being perpetually harrassed—by the Soviets and also by the Anglo-Americans. It was forced to make choices that it would have preferred to avoid: Obsessed by national independence after more than four years of occupation, it found itself at the beginning of the 1950s having to give up some of that independence.

This study will deal particularly with the question evoked by John W. Young:[13] How did France become a member of the Atlantic Alliance in 1949 after having signed a treaty of friendship with the Soviet Union less than five years previously? This causes one to question why France, as a Western power, went into an alliance with the Soviet Union in the first place (although France had had a close relationship with the predecessor regime of Czarist Russia dating back to 1893).

The signposts along the road that led from the Victory to NATO were the four pacts that France signed during this period—Moscow (December 1944), Dunkirk (March 1947), Brussels (March 1948), and Washington (April 1949)—at the end of which the ancient alliance between France and Russia (entered into originally with the 1893 pact directed against Germany) was definitely put to rest.

Though the French-Soviet treaty of 1944 was not formally denounced by Moscow until May 1955 at the moment when Germany, with French acquiescence, entered NATO, France had already joined a collective security pact aimed implicitly, to say the least, against the Soviet Union. And this pact, the North Atlantic Treaty signed in Washington on April 4, 1949, was to be followed a year and a half later by France joining in an integrated defense of Western Europe under an American general—the Supreme Allied Commander, Europe (SACEUR). In entering this system, France gave up a degree of its own national sovereignty.

It was not only a question of sovereignty for the eleven other nations that joined with the United States in the Atlantic Alliance. It was a question of the unity of Europe. This was to be held in check, at least in part, by the seemingly permanent entry of the United States into European affairs from 1947–1948 onwards. John Foster Dulles, who was in the opposition at the time, and therefore could speak freely, had the following remark to make before the U.S. Senate in 1949, as noted by Lawrence Kaplan: "The Economic Recovery Act [Marshall Plan] and the North Atlantic Treaty were the two things that prevented a unity of Europe which in the long run may be more valuable than either of them."[14]

As the European world split into two blocs in 1947–1948, France, which had been liberated by the Anglo-Americans, naturally fell on the Western side. But within the Western camp, France was the least amenable to the idea of a revived Germany as part of a European security system, an idea that came to be favored by its two allies. France's intransigeance on German economic recovery began to change with the inception of the European Coal and Steel Community idea in 1950; its resistance to German rearmament only effectively disappeared with the admission of Germany into NATO in 1955.

Postwar Germany, swept by a pacifism that has hardly diminished to this day, did not become the revisionist power that so many French people feared. Instead, a contrary trend developed: France, while not dominating Germany in the strict sense, held an ascendancy over Germany for forty-five years until the latter's reunification in 1990. It was as though, in a curious displacement of time, the wave of pacifism that gripped France in the interwar period (and which became discredited in France as a result of the war) transferred itself to Germany after World War II.[15]

As the 1950s wore on, this French ascendancy was accompanied by a complicity that was to belie the harsh and trauma-laden policy of France toward Germany in the postwar period. It was as though France had renewed its continental vocation. It was as though the seventy-five-year period of Germany's aggressive eruption in Europe had receded, and France could return—albeit cautiously—to its traditional preoccupation with a multi-polar continent in equilibrium.

Moreover, the British-French alliance of the prewar period was never able satisfactorily to be put back together again. Writ finis on the beach at Dunkirk in May–June 1940 in Marc Bloch's poignant story of "this French liaison officer assigned to a British regiment who, after several months of comradeship in the cantonment and in combat, was abandoned on the beach, barred from getting aboard a ship as he watched his friends of the day before climb up the gangway."[16] The alliance was smashed to pieces in the ruthless—but probably necessary—British attack on the French fleet at Mers-el-Kebir on July 3, 1940, in which 1,300 French sailors lost their lives.

As for the United States, it was, by French definition, an Anglo-Saxon country and therefore by extension an element in the historic competition between France and England. The widespread use of the term "Anglo-Saxon" in France, alternately startling and irritating to Americans, is a mark of the celebrated French "difference." For there is one thing that France has always confidently known that it is not: Anglo-Saxon.

And though the United States, like France, was a republic, it did not, as Furet put it, have the same status, rituals, and traditions as France and Britain, these two most ancient countries of Europe: "If, at the hour of victory [in World War II], Europe had more than ever need of America, it retained its old habit of not taking into account the regime of the United

States. . . . Even the war of [19]14–18] had not broken down the condescension of old Europe toward [the United States]."[17]

What the United States did have, however, was its feared—and sometimes hated—power, which the United States would come to exercise, as
the postwar threat from the Soviet Union became all-absorbing and the
American presence indispensable, with increasing assurance and its own
brand of condescension.

NOTES

1. François Furet, *Le passé d'une illusion: essai sur l'idée communiste au XXe
siècle* (Paris: Robert Laffont/Calmann-Lévy, 1995), 443. The "healer," of course,
is Charles de Gaulle.

2. Ibid., 443–44. The quotation from Raymond Aron is from the book *Le Spec-
tateur engagé* (Paris: Julliard, 1981), 110. Jules Roy was a World War II Resistance
figure and writer who contributed articles to *La France libre*, a journal that Aron
helped run from London after the fall of France. His latest work, published in
1996, is entitled "Adieu ma mère, adieu mon coeur."

3. Stanley Hoffmann, "The Trauma of 1940," in *La France des années noires,
vol. I, De la défaite à Vichy*, ed. Jean-Pierre Azéma and François Bédarida (Paris:
Plon, 1993), 137.

4. Ibid., 136–37.

5. Charles de Gaulle, *Lettres, Notes et Carnets*, vol. II (Paris: Plon, 1981), 30.

6. William L. Langer, ed., *An Encyclopedia of World History* (Boston: Houghton Mifflin, 1972), 951.

7. Robert O. Paxton and Nicholas Wahl, eds., *De Gaulle and the United States:
A Centennial Reappraisal* (Providence, R.I.: Berg, 1993), 334.

8. Remarks at a panel entitled "Appeasement the 1930s: Right or Wrong Policy?" at the annual conference of the Society of French Historical Studies held at
Boston University on March 22, 1990.

9. Charles de Gaulle, *Discours et Messages, vol. I, Pendant la guerre, Juin 1940–
Janvier 1946* (Paris: Plon, 1970), 623. (From a speech at Strasbourg on October 5,
1945.)

10. Furet, *Le passé d'une illusion*, 443.

11. Ibid.

12. Ibid., 416.

13. See the Preface to *France, the Cold War and the Western Alliance* (Leicester,
U.K.: Leicester University Press, 1990).

14. Lawrence S. Kaplan, *NATO and the United States: The Enduring Alliance*
(Boston: Twayne, 1988), 26. (The citation is from *North Atlantic Treaty Hearings*,
Senate Committee on Foreign Relations, 81 Cong., 1st sess. [Washington, D.C.:
GPO, 1949], 2: 368–69.)

15. "The war finally dishonored pacifism [in France], so powerful in 1939" (Furet, *Le passé d'une illusion*, 448).

16. Marc Bloch, *L'étrange défaite* (Paris: Albin Michel, 1957), 102.

17. Furet, *Le passé d'une illusion*, 419.

PART ONE

CHAPTER 1

The "Russian Hope" and Its Disappointments

France, for its part, does not accommodate itself to this rigid confrontation of two [Blocs]. Without ceasing—quite the contrary—to be par excellence a country of liberty and a Western nation, [France] would like to see the unhealthy charm broken and, at least as far as she is concerned, that a process be launched with the European states of the "East," aimed at détente, entente and cooperation.

Obviously, she would like to achieve this in the first instance with the Soviet Union. The reasons for this primordial choice are evident. In effect Russia is in all respects the principal power in the region of the world where she is located. What is more, she seems to France an interlocutor with whom comprehension and collaboration are eminently natural. There exists a political and affective reality as old as our two countries, which has to do with their history and their geography, and the fact that no fundamental grievance has ever opposed them, even in the times of "War and Peace" or in the epoch of Sebastopol; and finally with the affinities which are clearly evident, both at the level of their elites . . . as well [with] the peoples themselves. It is self-evident that their alliance in the world wars, and particularly the capital part which the Soviet Union played in the decisive victory which crowned the Second [one], have only reinforced, with the French, this sentiment of solidarity.

Charles de Gaulle, 1966[1]

In a letter to Paul Claudel[2] in December 1950, Charles de Gaulle gave expression to the notion of a central role for France in the Europe of the postwar period, albeit in characteristically presumptuous terms:

Once there appeared the signs of United States direct action in Europe in 1941, I tried, with my terribly reduced means, to get American policymakers to recognize that it was in their interest to have a dialogue with Europe—which at the time meant essentially Free France. The repressed passions of Roosevelt, the intrigues of the British, the ambiguous [status] of Vichy, prevented things from turning out that way. The result was Teheran, Yalta, Potsdam.[3]

On the one hand, this passage can be looked at as the quintessence of Gaullist megalomania. For what was Free France at its origins but an idea in the mind of Charles de Gaulle? And what would Free France represent without him? The answer, of course, was nothing, or next to nothing. But looked at from another angle, we return to the fact, mentioned in the Introduction, that of all the countries conquered by Germany, France was by far the most important. Because France was the biggest of the continental countries, and the one with the longest tradition of statehood, it was natural that France should be the American interlocutor for continental Europe after the war.

This France-centered thinking, this sort of national nombrilism, was not confined to the lofty mind of Charles de Gaulle. It permeated the Gaullist movement. According to information released in 1996 by the National Security Agency, based on intercepts of Free French diplomatic messages in the period 1943–1944, a remarkably similar analysis was being made by the Free French delegate in Moscow, Roger Garreau, this time with a view toward *Russian* foreign policy:

[Russia] is "still haunted by the specter of encirclement by hostile capitalistic powers." Determined not to find herself "once more isolated at the close of this war as she was at the time of the Munich crisis," and to shield herself from "this danger which has obsessed her" for more than a score of years, "she must have in western Europe a power sufficiently strong and independent to serve as a guarantee of her security." . . . "This power can be none other than France, provided that this France is not Vichy France," as she "realizes that the friendship of France would be the best guarantee."[4]

Franklin Roosevelt, to say the least, did not share this Free French optic. As Max Ascoli, in his introduction to the papers of one of Roosevelt's key advisors, Adolph A. Berle, Jr., pointed out: "In their antagonism toward the Free French movement and Charles de Gaulle personally, the President, Berle, and most of official Washington went to the extreme. It took time for many authoritative people to get rid of the notion: there was no France."[5]

Curiously, this was not an opinion that was fully shared by the American public or the press. For the very influential journalist of the period, Walter Lippmann, "France was always, and indiscutably, one of the great powers," according to Ronald Steel. Lippmann was of the opinion that "no question of European politics or security could be decided without

France.''[6] Soon after the French defeat, Lippmann wrote on September 17, 1940, that "we must not think that the rest of Europe, which has always looked toward France, is not watching how we treat France today.''[7]

The contrast is striking between, on the one hand, the Gaullist *Weltanschauung*, in which Europe meant essentially continental Europe, and in which Britain was only rarely included in such a context and, on the other hand, the casual and legendary dismissal of France by Franklin Roosevelt. According to Henry Kissinger, in his book *Diplomacy*, "[Franklin] Roosevelt vastly overestimated the postwar capacities of Great Britain by asking it to handle simultaneously the defense and the reconstruction of Europe. Great Britain's position in this scheme was all the more overblown because of Roosevelt's deep disdain for France.''[8]

De Gaulle had few illusions about Anglo-American intentions and the obstacles he could expect his two allies to place in his way. In a message of October 11, 1942, he wrote the following to Gen. Georges Catroux[9] in Beirut: "The main goal at the moment is to exist, I repeat to exist, with all the means at our disposal. Later we shall see whether we have an interest in working with the British or with the Americans.''[10]

By contrast, and as the war continued to widen, de Gaulle nurtured the hope that the Russians would help him cope with the pressures that the British and Americans were placing on the Free French movement. In May 1942, he wrote to Free French leaders in various posts abroad that

a new and favorable element [in the situation] . . . is the attitude of Russia. The Soviets are well informed on the state of mind of the French population, are chronically irritated by the hesitations of the Anglo-Saxons, and [are] very disposed to support us diplomatically because the restoration of a great and strong France is essential to their future policy.[11]

(As Prof. Stanley Hoffmann observed, the long-term view of General de Gaulle was remarkably accurate, but in the short range it was less so. Seen through this lens, the words of May 1942 capture less the atmosphere of the 1940s than the 1960s, when the Soviets saw in France a useful counterweight to the Anglo-Americans and viewed the Gaullist regime in Paris as important to their policy.)

But the "Russian hope" of Charles de Gaulle, as expressed in the May 1942 message, turned out to be a false hope. The Soviet Union was no more disposed than the Roosevelt administration to recognize the position of France as that of a virtual great power. France at the time was not only too weak to count for much in the eyes of the Russians, but it also constituted a potential threat in the future. This is evident through documents recently brought to light by the Woodrow Wilson Center in Washington,[12] particularly in a memorandum by Ivan Maisky, dated January 10, 1944, shortly after his return to Moscow following a tour in London as ambas-

6 Forced to Choose

sador. This memorandum, addressed to Foreign Minister Viatcheslav Molotov, ran to forty double-spaced pages and set out the lines of a recommended foreign policy for the Soviet Union for the next thirty to fifty years.[13]

According to Maisky, the first objective to be achieved in the decades to come was to prevent Germany from committing aggression again. This would have to be accomplished through an occupation by the wartime allies of approximately ten years; by the dismemberment of the country; by its military, industrial, and ideological disarmament; by reparations; and by what Maisky called "re-education."[14]

Maisky put forward as a second strategic objective (and this sounds strangely like the famous Wolfowitz report of 1991, leaked from the Pentagon but then quickly disavowed as being only a draft)

[that of] preventing the formation in Europe of a power or a combination of powers possessing strong armies. Our interest will be best served if Europe in the postwar period has only one land power—the Soviet Union—and one maritime power—England. [Thus it is desirable] that France be restored but not to the level of its former military power.[15]

It is worth noting in passing, and in the light of these Soviet documents, that non-Russians have a tendency to forget, today as well as in the period at hand, that the great preoccupation of the Russians is in the area of security: how to assure a glacis along their western frontier. Just as non-French have a tendency to forget that the great obsession of the French, now as in the postwar period, is that national independence, lost in 1940, must never be lost again.

Thus, the Soviet leaders, at the approach of the end of the Second World War, sought first and foremost to ensure their security on the Soviet western frontier. They did not have the impression that the alliance with the Western powers was going to break up, although they suspected that the United States, to quote from Maisky's report, "could cause us problems, by stimulating the recovery of Germany and Japan . . . and by creating an anti-Soviet bloc in Europe, using countries such as France."[16]

The Soviet leaders anticipated that Western Europe of the postwar period would experience the natural emergence of governments of the "Popular Front" type,[17] a development that would fit best with the policy of the Soviet Union. The Soviets, as seen through these documents, seemed to recognize that in the final analysis, Western Europe was not part of their sphere of influence.

The Soviet documents, that of Maisky, and also those of Andrei Gromyko, particularly a long report of July 14, 1944, also addressed to Molotov,[18] are striking from at least three points of view. First, the Soviet leaders assumed a continuation of cooperative relations with the Anglo-

Americans after the war. Second, they perceived the possibility of differences between the British and the Americans after the war, especially in terms of economic competition. Third, they seemed to overestimate the power and the role of Great Britain. At the same time, they recognized that the British would be weakened as a result of the war and would therefore have to pursue a "conservative imperialism," attempting to hold on to what they had.[19]

With regard to the British, the Soviet point of view was not appreciably different from that of the Americans. As we have seen earlier in this chapter (see page 5), Franklin Roosevelt had an exaggerated notion of what Britain would represent in the future. On February 8, 1944, Roosevelt wrote to Winston Churchill with that curious combination of pretention and naïveté noted by André Fontaine:[20] "I am absolutely unwilling to police France and possibly Italy and the Balkans as well. After all, France is your baby and will take a lot of nursing in order to bring it to the point of walking alone."[21]

THE FRENCH-SOVIET TREATY OF DECEMBER 1944

As the war moved toward its end, Charles de Gaulle continued to rely on his "Russian hope," a hope that was to culminate in the Treaty of Alliance and Mutual Assistance, signed between France and the Soviet Union in December 1944. The general moved quickly: Less than two months after the long-delayed recognition of the French Provisional Government by the Anglo-Americans and the Soviets on October 23, de Gaulle undertook an extended visit to Russia. The visit culminated with the signing of the treaty on December 10—the first such treaty signed by the new French government.

Thus, at the moment of the Victory, France, which had fought on the Allied side on the Western front, linked itself in a defensive pact with the Soviet Union and with no other country. This was despite the fact that, until the formation of the French Committee of National Liberation in June 1943, Great Britain was the only outside power to have financed the Free French movement. At that point, when the payments stopped, the British Treasury had advanced to the movement nearly 35 million pounds.[22]

De Gaulle had expressly refused an offer by Winston Churchill to enter into a tripartite pact with Britain, France, and the Soviet Union—an offer made, with some maladresse, through Marshal Stalin and communicated to de Gaulle by the Soviets during his Russian visit.[23] (On the other hand, before the event de Gaulle had not discussed with his erstwhile patron, Churchill, his intention to visit Moscow.)

The essential fact, however, was that Churchill's proposal did not accord with de Gaulle's strategic objectives. "From the point of view of France,"

the general told Stalin, "the French-Soviet alliance is . . . of primordial importance."[24] Historically, de Gaulle explained to Stalin, "Great Britain has
great difficulty in acting preventively and in acting immediately [in Eu-
rope]."[25] Elaborating further, de Gaulle said,

We much prefer a system of security in three stages:
[first stage], French-Soviet pact;
[second stage], Anglo-Soviet and Anglo-French pacts;
[third stage], collective security (with the inclusion of America).[26]

An Anglo-French treaty was far from being a top priority in de Gaulle's
eyes—all the more so in that there were serious problems to settle with
Britain, particularly in the Levant. But more fundamentally, de Gaulle had
few illusions about the duration of French-British cooperation. As he
wrote following Churchill's visit to Paris in November 1944,

It was apparent that England favored France's political reappearance, that she
would continue to do so for reasons of equilibrium, tradition and security, that
she desired a formal alliance with us, but would not consent to link her strategy
with ours, believing herself in a position to function independently between Moscow and Washington.[27]

This was a function that de Gaulle had cut out for himself, and for
France—an independent role in dealing with Moscow and with Washing-
ton. For de Gaulle, the priority was in the German marches to the east of
France—the Rhineland, the Ruhr, and the Saar—where he hoped to find
Russian support for his claims in return for the Treaty of Alliance and
Mutual Assistance of December 1944.

Jean Laloy, the interpreter who accompanied General de Gaulle during
his visit to Russia in December 1944, made much of two compromises
made by the general to his hosts. First of all, de Gaulle signed restrictive
articles of the type also signed by the Czechs, the Yugoslavs, and the Poles
in their treaties with the Russians concluded in the 1943–1945 period;[28]
specifically, two articles of the French-Russian treaty taken together (Articles 2 and 4) call on each party to support the other in a case where the
latter became implicated in the future in hostilities with Germany, either
following an aggression by the latter, or for having taken "all measures
necessary to eliminate any new threat from Germany."[29]

Secondly, noted Laloy, de Gaulle agreed to send an unofficial representative to the Soviet-sponsored Lublin Government in Poland.[30] On the first
of these two points, one could observe that General de Gaulle, in spite of
a marked and almost unhealthy intransigeance, knew nevertheless how to
choose the right moment to come to a compromise. On the second point,

it should be noted that the French Provisional Government, even before the Moscow Conference, had intended to send Christian Fouchet to Lublin as a sort of unofficial representative to uphold French interests and the French point of view at the moment of the liberation of Poland.[31]

It should also be noted in passing that the summary and at times brutal manner in which de Gaulle treated people caused in them an inevitable loss of objectivity. Laloy comes to mind, as does also Georges Bidault, who, in the words of the French ambassador to London, Mr. René Massigli, "had felt as a test the months served under the authority—he would willingly have said the iron rule—of the general."[32] Bidault, who held the Foreign Affairs portfolio from November 1944 until July 1948 and who later briefly became prime minister, played a significant role in French policy during this period.

If, at the time of the signing of the French-Soviet treaty of December 1944, de Gaulle had given in on the point of official recognition of the Lublin Government, Stalin might have been more obliged to him because the Soviet leader would thereby have been able to drive a wedge in the Allied position on the key question of the postwar status of Poland. And in this manner Stalin would have been able to ensure more rapidly his glacis in the West.

However, de Gaulle did not cede to the Russians on Poland, notwithstanding the contrary thesis of Jean Laloy. France did not recognize the postwar Polish government until June 1945, at the same time as the Allies. This was well after the Yalta Conference, at which France was absent and during which the Anglo-Americans had ceded ground all along the line on Poland—the country for which Great Britain and France had gone to war in the first place. According to the Yalta Accords, the London Polish Government would be represented only up to 25 percent in the new Cabinet, thus guaranteeing its eclipse over time by the Lublin faction.

In the immediate aftermath of World War II, Poland represented the one great failing of the Anglo-Americans. The war had been started to preserve Poland's integrity, and now the country was inexorably falling under the control of a Communist dictatorship directed from Moscow. The only thing the Poles received at Yalta was the poisoned gift of the German lands in Silesia and East Prussia—an action that gravely compromised the relations between Germany and Poland for decades.

And so, at the moment when World War II was near its end, de Gaulle was clearly disposed to a close association with Russia. He hoped, if not expected, to become an important partner with the Soviet Union in the deliberations over the fate of Germany in the following years. But Stalin did not share the same perspective. From his point of view, France had not contributed much during the war, and in this sense, he was more in tune with Roosevelt than with Churchill. At the Yalta Conference, as Henry Kissinger has written, Roosevelt, in the presence of Stalin, chided

Churchill for having tried "artificially" to make France into a strong power.[33]

One cannot say with certainty that de Gaulle actually envisaged, in megalomaniaical fashion, a sort of "grand bargain" with Stalin in December 1944—on the one hand the Soviets would take part of Poland and the Poles would be given compensating territories in Germany, and on the other hand France would advance to its "natural frontier" on the Rhine. But apparently de Gaulle nourished the hope of getting something in the West out of his dealings with the Russians. In his memoirs, Vincent Auriol, president of the Fourth Republic from 1947 to 1953, alluded to this: He maintained that he tried in vain to persuade de Gaulle to sign a three-way treaty with the Soviet Union and Great Britain, that a recommendation he made in his capacity as President of the Foreign Affairs Committee of the Consultative Assembly in 1945. De Gaulle did not take up the suggestion, according to Auriol, because he wanted to see if he could receive satisfaction for French claims to the left bank of the Rhine in return for signing a bilateral treaty with the Soviets.[34]

In this "année noire," which 1945 was for de Gaulle, France was excluded from three conferences: Yalta in February, Potsdam in July–August, and Moscow in December. The latter concerned the peace treaties for the satellite allies of Germany: Rumania, Bulgaria, Hungary, and Finland. Soviet intentions regarding the latter peace treaties had already been made known at the intervening conference at London (September 11–October 2) of the Big Five (the USSR, the United States, Great Britain, France, and China): The Soviets did not want France to be a partner in these Eastern European treaties.[35]

But despite these setbacks, the underlying reality was different. France's long-range position had been restored. As Erik Conan observed, "France recovered as though by a miracle of History its sovereignty and its international positions and saw itself given a seat as a permanent member of the UN Security Council."[36]

What is more, France was given a minor but blocking position in decisions concerning the future of Germany. If it felt strong enough to use it, it had a veto power as a member of the Allied Control Commission, which sat at Berlin and which was empowered to decide on all questions concerning Germany. As an example of the blocking position that France enjoyed, there was the case of the Saar, which had voted 90.8 percent in favor of its recission to Germany in 1935,[37] but which did not become a part of the postwar Federal Republic of Germany until January 1, 1957.

The minor position that the French got in Germany after the war—a small occupation zone carved out of the British and American Zones—was nevertheless substantial, considering their quasi-absence from the war, or from most of it. None of this would have been possible without the towering figure of de Gaulle, representing the new France emerging from the war. If de Gaulle had not been in power in Paris in 1944–1945, France would not have had a "blocking" role in the occupation of Germany and almost certainly would not have become a permanent member of the UN Security Council.

The role of Churchill in this "accident of history" must also be acknowledged. It was his intercession at the Yalta Conference in favor of France's position in the United Nations and vis-à-vis Germany that was critical. In contrast to Stalin, Churchill saw in France an ally of considerable potential importance in a weakened Europe. And in contrast to Roosevelt, Churchill was more realistic in his political judgment. (The same cannot be said for Churchill as a military strategist—witness his quixotic quest for an Allied military thrust into Yugoslavia, which, as some observers have noted, could have led to a north-south instead of an east-west division in Europe, with Soviet troops advancing to the English Channel!)

Churchill reasoned that he would have need of France in the occupation of Germany after the departure of American troops from Europe, which seemed inevitable at the time.[38] Also, for Churchill, France was an important potential ally who could assist in preventing the advance of the Soviets into Western Europe. Thus it was Churchill, alone among the Big Three wartime leaders, who pushed for a peacetime role for France as a virtual great power. It was not surprising, therefore, to hear this assertion about Churchill from Jean-Marcel Jeanneney[39] at the 1990 conference on General de Gaulle in New York: "Maybe the only man for whom, in spite of their differences, [de Gaulle] had real affection was Winston Churchill, because, unlike others, he welcomed and understood de Gaulle as early as June 1940 and gave him the means, albeit limited, to begin his action."[40]

Somewhat like Churchill, but in quite different circumstances, de Gaulle left the political scene shortly after the Victory. But in contrast to Churchill, whose Conservative Party was repudiated by the voters in July 1945, representing a personal blow for Sir Winston, de Gaulle did not have a political party and thus was not rejected by the people.[41] Rather, de Gaulle was immobilized by the political parties that had emerged from the French Resistance; one could say that his resignation represented, in a certain way, the triumph of the internal resistance over the external resistance. Both of these wartime leaders, Churchill and de Gaulle, had constantly demanded sacrifices of their people, and thus they both experienced a phenomenon of rejection at the war's end. The French, at the time, were clearly more in a mood for *jouissance* (pleasure) than for sacrifice.

Before the departure of de Gaulle from power in January 1946, the Soviets had not shown hostility toward his regime.[42] Indeed there had been a sort of surface complicity. In December 1944, at their meeting in Moscow, Stalin and de Gaulle spoke of Maurice Thorez, the leader of the French Communist Party, who had fled France after the Nazi-Soviet Pact and the start of the hostilities and had spent the war years in the Soviet Union. He had returned to France in late 1944 with de Gaulle's permission. Stalin said to de Gaulle: "In my opinion, he is a good Frenchman. If I were in your place, I would not put him in prison." Then he added with a smile, "At least not right away." De Gaulle, little given to light conversation about such matters, replied, "The French government treats Frenchmen according to the services it expects of them."[43]

In fact, Thorez was to render signal service to the government of General de Gaulle, particularly in agreeing to the dissolution of the Communist-dominated resistance militias formed during the war. But de Gaulle was to make a historic compromise in November 1945, when he brought five Communist ministers into his government, at the head of whom was Thorez. However, the Communists remained fiercely opposed (as did others) to de Gaulle's vision for a new French constitution, in which they detected a Caesarism in sharp contradiction with the tradition of the French Revolution, which gave all powers to Parliament.

Unable to obtain a constitution of his liking or, one could say, of his stature, de Gaulle resigned in January 1946. His surprise move took place in the midst of efforts by a Constituent Assembly to draft a new constitution to take the place of that of the defunct Third Republic (1875–1940). After one rejection in June 1946, the voters finally approved a second draft in October 1946. In January 1947, Vincent Auriol was elected president of the new Fourth Republic with powers not very different from those of his predecessors. Governmental instability and parliamentary rule had returned to France.[44]

Once installed in the presidency, Auriol vainly tried to establish a personal relationship with de Gaulle. He invited the general and his wife to the Elysée Palace for an informal visit, a sort of "housewarming" just among the two couples. But de Gaulle, with little taste for friendly small talk with opposing political figures, declined politely but firmly. He replied, "I greatly appreciate your invitation. But I cannot accept it, as my visits to Paris always cause commotion. I prefer not to."[45]

There is little question that de Gaulle thought he would be quickly called back to power by the people, to rescue what was widely perceived as a deadlocked political system. He alluded to this in a letter he wrote less than two months after his resignation: "Whatever indignation one feels, we must consider that the future, and a near future, will return things to their proper place."[46]

De Gaulle was wrong. He had to wait twelve years, until the moment when it was seen that the political system was leading France into a civil war over Algeria. For the time being, however, the French people were not yet ready to give up what de Gaulle referred to as the "games, poisons and delights"[47] of French parliamentary democracy—however harmful that was to the image of France in the world.

U.S. VIEW OF DE GAULLE AS UN-DEMOCRATIC

It is one of the oddities of history that Charles de Gaulle—described by Furet as one of the two greatest antifascists of Europe who were later to be at the point of the anti-Communist struggle in Europe (the other was Winston Churchill)[48]—was not particularly perceived by the United States as a bulwark against Communism in France. Rather, he was seen as a quasi-fascist or Caesarist figure who was liable, as were the Communists, to undermine French democracy.

With the re-emergence of the traditional political parties in France toward the end of the war, the United States focused its attention and support on three parties: the Socialists, the Radicals, and especially the new Christian Democratic party known as the Mouvement Républicain Populaire (MRP). This bloc of parties hopefully was to constitute a "Third Force" between the Communists and the Gaullists. When the Communists were dismissed from the Cabinet in May 1947, and these "Third Force" parties, in addition to some independents, constituted the new governing coalition, the U.S. Ambassador in Paris, Jefferson Caffery, cabled Washington that

the party composition of the present government is from our viewpoint the best that could be hoped for . . . it excludes the Communists on the extreme left and the reactionary elements on the right, and combines the fundamentally democratic forces of the center and the left which still represent the views and command the support of a majority of the French Parliament and people despite a general public feeling of disillusionment with government fumbling and incoherence.[49]

A Communist victory in France, Caffery added, would greatly facilitate Soviet penetration in the region and would have grave consequences for the U.S. position in Germany, whereas a Gaullist victory would make the continuation of democracy in France problematic.[50]

Thus, while General de Gaulle was fulminating against the Communists as being under the orders of a "foreign enterprise of domination, directed by the masters of a 'great Slavic power' "[51] was boldly taunting them as "separatists," and was responding in kind to Communist strong-arm tactics at political rallies, he was largely dismissed by U.S. authorities as a sort of avatar of Napoléon Bonaparte.

The problem with the "Third Force" coalition was that it was a weak reed for the United States to support, as was glaringly revealed in the municipal elections of October 1947. The new Gaullist party formed that spring, the Rally of the French People (RFP), won nearly 40 percent of the vote, while the Communists held firm at 30 percent. This meant that seven out of ten Frenchmen did not support the ruling coalition favored by the United States. At a time when Europe had begun splitting into two blocs, this coalition, led by Resistance leaders of the non-Communist left and the Christian Democratic center, was again and again to disappoint the hopes that the United States placed in it.

NOTES

1. Charles de Gaulle, *Discours et Messages (DM), vol. V, Vers le terme, Février 1966–Avril 1969* (Paris: Omnibus/Plon, 1970), 462. The reference to Tolstoy's *War and Peace* is an allusion to the Napoleonic Wars; similarly, Sebastopol refers to the Crimean War (1854–1855). In each case France and Russia were opponents.

2. French poet, playwright, and ambassador; member of the Académie française.

3. Charles de Gaulle, *Lettres, Notes et Carnets* (LNC) vol. 6 (Paris: Plon, 1981), 461.

4. *National Archives II*, Pacific Strategic Intelligence Section, "French-Russian Relations, September 1943–December 1944" (PSIS 400–7), April 11, 1945, 2.

5. *Navigating the Rapids, 1918–1971*, from the papers of Adolph A. Berle, edited by B. B. Berle and T. B. Jacobs (New York: Harcourt Brace Jovanovich, 1973), xxvi.

6. Ronald Steel, "Walter Lippmann and Charles de Gaulle," in *De Gaulle and the United States: A Centennial Reappraisal*, ed. (Oxford/Providence: Berg, 1994), 378.

7. Ibid.

8. Henry Kissinger, *Diplomacy* (New York: Simon and Schuster, 1994), 396.

9. Governor-General of Indochina in 1940, Catroux was the most senior of French military officers who rallied to de Gaulle. In 1941, he was named Free French High Commissioner in the Levant, at Beirut.

10. LNC, vol. 4 (1982), 411.

11. Ibid., 271.

12. See in particular Vladimir O. Pechatnov, "The Big Three after World War II," *Cold War International History Project* Working Paper No. 13 (Washington, D.C.: Woodrow Wilson Center, 1995).

13. Ibid., 2.

14. Ibid., 2–3.

15. Ibid., 3.

16. Ibid., 6.

17. These were coalition governments of the type that appeared in the 1930s in France and Spain. In France, the coalition, formed in 1936, was composed of the Socialists, the Communists, and the Radicals, though the Communists did not participate in the government as ministers.

18. Pechatnov, "The Big Three after World War II," pp. 6–9.

19. Ibid., 5.

20. André Fontaine, *Histoire de la Guerre Froide, vol. I, De la Révolution d'Octobre à la Guerre de Corée, 1917–1950* (Paris: Fayard, 1965), 261.

21. Alfred D. Chandler, Jr., ed., *The Papers of Dwight David Eisenhower, vol. III, The War Years* (Baltimore, Md.: The Johns Hopkins Press, 1970), 1727.

22. G. E. Maguire, *Anglo-American Policy Towards the Free French* (New York: St. Martin's Press, 1995), 117.

23. Charles de Gaulle, *The Complete War Memoirs of Charles de Gaulle, vol. III, Salvation 1944–1946*, trans. Richard Howard (New York: Simon and Schuster, 1964), 76.

24. Charles de Gaulle, *Mémoires de Guerre, vol. III, Le salut 1944–1946* (Paris: Plon/Presses Pocket, 1959), 407.

25. Ibid.

26. Ibid., 408.

27. De Gaulle, *War Memoirs*, 3: 60.

28. Jean Laloy, *Yalta: Yesterday, Today, Tomorrow*, trans. William R. Tyler (New York: Harper and Row, 1988), 58.

29. De Gaulle, *Mémoires de Guerre*, 3: 411. (Text of the French-Soviet Treaty.)

30. Late in the war, the Soviets formed a pro-Communist Polish exile government in Lublin, Poland, as a counterweight to the pro-Allied Polish government-in-exile, which had set itself up in London after the German invasion of 1939.

31. John W. Young, *France, the Cold War and the Western Alliance* (Leicester, U.K.: Leicester University Press, 1990), 31.

32. René Massigli, *Une comédie des erreurs* (Paris: Plon, 1978), 97.

33. Kissinger, *Diplomacy*, 396.

34. Vincent Auriol, *Journal du septennat*, vol. I, 1947 (Paris: Armand Colin, 1970), 17–18.

35. Georges-Henri Soutou, "La securité de la France dans l'après-guerre," in *La France et l'OTAN, 1949–1996*, ed. Maurice Vaïsse, Pierre Mélandri, and Frédéric Bozo (Brussels: Éditions Complexe, 1996), 25. As Professor Soutou noted, "Despite the [December 1944] pact, the relations with Moscow had been disappointing all through the year 1945." (Ibid.)

36. Erik Conan, "Contre Vichy: le prix de l'honneur," *L'Express*, 2 novembre 1995, xii.

37. Alfred Grosser, *L'Allemagne en Occident: la République fédérale 40 ans après* (Paris: Fayard, 1985), 42.

38. Fontaine, *Guerre Froide*, 1: 269.

39. Jean-Marcel Jeanneney was the son of Jules Jeanneney, the president of the French Senate in 1940 and who became a supporter of General de Gaulle.

40. Paxton and Wahl, *De Gaulle and the United States: A Centennial Reappraisal*, 230.

41. In 1943, a Gaullist Resistance leader, Pierre Brossolette, recommended to the general that he form a mass party at the war's end, before the prewar parties had a chance to reorganize themselves. De Gaulle may have regretted not having done this, according to his confidant, Alain Peyrefitte, who discussed this with the general in 1966. (Alain Peyrefitte, *C'était de Gaulle* [Paris: Fayard, 1994], 33). Brossolette, later captured and tortured by the Gestapo, elected to commit suicide rather than give up secrets. This he did by jumping out of a fifth floor window at Gestapo Headquarters on Avenue Foch in Paris.

42. De Gaulle had the foresight in 1942 to create the Normandy squadron, later to be known as the Normandy-Niemen squadron, which was the only foreign unit per se to have fought as part of the Soviet Air Force during World War II.

43. De Gaulle, *War Memoirs*, 3: 71–72.

44. See Charles Cogan, *Oldest Allies, Guarded Friends: The United States and France since 1940* (Westport, CT and London: Praeger, 1994), 55–56.

45. Auriol, *Journal du septennat*, 1: 31.

46. LNC vol. 6 (1984), 192. (Letter to Mdm. Hélène Terre, commander of the women's section of Free French Volunteers. The activities of Mdm. Terre's group during the war had been criticized by some elements of the press.)

47. Charles de Gaulle, "Renewal, 1958–1962," part 1 of *Memoirs of Hope: Renewal and Endeavor*, trans. Terence Kilmartin (New York: Simon and Schuster, 1971), 277.

48. François Furet, *Le passé d' une illusion: essai sur l'idée communiste au XXe siècle* (Paris: Robert Laffont/Calmann-Lévy, 1995), 475.

49. *Foreign Relations of the United States* (FRUS) (1947), vol. 3 (Washington, D.C.: Government Printing Office, 1972), 709.

50. Ibid., 712.

51. Charles de Gaulle, *Discours et Messages, vol. II, Dans l'attente, Février 1946– Avril 1959* (Paris: Plon, 1970), 99. (Speech at Rennes, July 27, 1947.)

CHAPTER 2

The Attempt at a Renewal of the Entente Cordiale

To my keen regret, the alliance between our two countries, perennially celebrated in official speeches, had scarcely any substance. . . . Great Britain would never have a margin of action sufficient to escape the supervision of the United States. . . . I would not exchange the construction of Europe, of which Federal Germany was an essentual pillar, for a French-British entente that would be desirable but would amount only to good intentions.

François Mitterrand to Margaret Thatcher, January 20, 1990[1]

On October 22, 1945, a French military officer, without realizing it, made a dazzling prediction of the shape of European security in the future. The officer, Col. Pierre Lassalle of the General Staff of National Defense (EMGDN), made this statement not as a prediction, however, but as a recommendation, which was approved by his chief, Gen. Alphonse Juin:

[There is a] necessity [for] a "permanent conventional equilibrium" in Europe, accompanied by a commitment on the part of the Allies to bring about an "integrated command" ("commandement unique") and the permanent presence, in this postwar period, of "450,000 Americans" within an organized ensemble "of the order of 50 divisions," with the "possible" participation of a West Germany duly controlled.[2]

In the immediate aftermath of the peace, such a statement would have been unthinkable in public discourse. In a secret staff study, where political considerations usually take second place to military realism, such projections are characteristic, though few have been as prescient as this one.

THE DUNKIRK TREATY OF ALLIANCE AND MUTUAL ASSISTANCE

At the moment of the Victory, although France in significant measure owed its position during the war and its attributions after the war to the good offices of Winston Churchill, it entered into an alliance solely with the Soviet Union—for reasons that had mainly to do with its obsessional fear of Germany.

Even in the best of times, relations between the cross-Channel partners, Britain and France, have never been easy. Geographic *voisinage* coupled with a cultural gulf; the memory of distant (and not so distant) battles dating from the dawn of these two ancient nations; and a long-time competition for empire between these two confined countries of Europe made for an endless potential for friction.

In the post–World War II period, a new element was added to this ancient rivalry: a psychological imbalance stemming from the fact that France had been defeated and occupied by Germany while Britain had not. Britain was considered, and considered itself, a great power well into the 1950s, until the bubble burst at Suez. France, weak and disheartened, oscillating between nihilism and revanchism, remained frozen in the status of virtual great power until the late 1950s when General de Gaulle stepped forward a second time to save the country from its own induced chaos.

On June 27, 1962, four years after returning to power, Charles de Gaulle reflected acidly on this cross-Channel relationship to his confidant, Alain Peyrefitte:

Our greatest hereditary enemy was not Germany, it was England. From the Hundred Years War to Fashoda, she hardly stopped struggling against us. And since that time she has had difficulty in not opposing her interests against ours. Look at the way she conducted herself during the two wars. She forbade us from reacting to the reoccupation of the Rhineland. She prevented us from opposing the rearmament of Germany. She abandoned us at Dunkirk. She joyfully shelled our fleet at Mers-el-Kebir. She betrayed us in Syria. She sides systematically with America. She wants to prevent us from succeeding with the Common Market. It is true that she was our ally during the two wars, but she is not naturally disposed to wish us well.

With Germany, on the other hand, it is clear that our interests meet, and will meet more and more. She needs us as much as we need her.[3]

But in the post–World War II period, the obsessional concern, including that of General de Gaulle, was with the German threat. Even when this threat rapidly lost all credibility, as it was obvious that Germany had been dealt a knockout blow, the threat became fixed in the French mind with an unreal fear, based on past experience with perceived German treachery, of an eventual Russo-German combination. It was the fear of a new

Rapallo, the treaty of cooperation signed between a defeated Germany and the Soviet Union in 1922. Only later would the focus of fear become wholly transferred to the Soviet Union. As Georges-Henri Soutou described it: "The transition from the perception of a German threat (considered the sole one at the time of the French-Soviet treaty of December 10, 1944) to the perception of a threat of a German-Soviet conjunction constituted an essential dialectic moment in the process of the French understanding of the Cold War."[4]

Whether the postwar German policy of France was conducted by Charles de Gaulle or by the governments that succeeded him, it could be described as focused on three objectives:

• That Germany never again pose a military threat to France
• That France be assured of its security on its eastern frontier with Germany
• That Germany not be allowed to recover economically more rapidly than France

Almost immediately, these French objectives came into conflict with those of the Anglo-Americans, who saw that Germany could not be left as a vaccuum in Central Europe. Soon, Washington and London set about building up Germany as a rampart against the Soviet threat.

Despite this clash of interests, France realized it could not afford to become isolated from its Western partners. Very weak militarily, with an increasing part of its army forced to fight a colonial war in Indochina,[5] and far from being restored to economic health, France was clearly in need of allies. The obvious choice was Britain, but beyond the general inhibition about reviving an alliance that had ended so painfully in 1940, the recrudescence of Anglo-French differences in the Levant in May 1946 and the lack of support by the British for French aims in Germany had served to freeze any further steps toward a rapprochement. Paradoxically, the British had sought to enhance their imperial interests in the Middle East at the expense of those of France, currying favor with the Arab world by encouraging independence for Syria and Lebanon; whereas in Indochina the British effect was the opposite: There the British served to enhance French imperial aims. Having no interests in Indochina, and fearing the effect of an independence movement in other areas of Southeast Asia and South Asia, especially British India, they assisted in the re-establishment of a French military presence in Indochina.

It was the Socialist Léon Blum, briefly prime minister of France's last provisional government (end 1946–beginning 1947), who seized the opportunity to fill the void in the Anglo-French relationship.

Perhaps it is too much to say that the genesis of the Treaty of Dunkirk, signed on March 4, 1947, between France and Great Britain, lay in a cabal of Anglophiles and Francophiles on either side of the Channel. However, this would not be very far off the mark. Blum, the key figure in this affair, and rather pro-British for a French political personality, accomplished the preliminary—and decisive—step during his brief stewardship as prime minister (December 16, 1949–January 16, 1947).

The "Dunkirk episode"—and it can be called such because it was an event without great consequence—began on December 28, 1946, with a conversation between Blum and the inveterate Francophile Duff Cooper, British ambassador in Paris.[6] Without his government's authorization, Ambassador Cooper proposed to the French prime minister that the gap represented by the absence of a treaty of mutual assistance between the two countries be filled.[7] It should be noted that the idea of closer links between the two countries was in the air, particularly now that France was emerging from the tentative status of having a provisional government: The Fourth Republic, created by the new constitution approved in October 1946, was to take effect in January 1947.[8]

As a result of the meeting with Cooper, Blum came up with the idea that he, as the last prime minister of the Provisional Government, might rectify the anomaly of France being linked by treaty with only one major power, the Soviet Union (although by this time the Treaty of Moscow of December 1944 had been emptied of some of its original significance).

At the same time, however, Blum recognized that France, in the midst of a very severe winter, would be unwise to conclude an agreement with Great Britain without a perception by the French public that it was receiving some benefit. Preferably this benefit would consist of increased deliveries of coal, which was critically lacking in France. This could come from the Ruhr, or from Britain. On December 31, 1946, Blum wrote a letter to Prime Minister Clement Attlee, and he had it hand-carried to London by Interior Minister Jules Moch, who was scheduled to engage in talks with the British on coal.[9]

Attlee was unable to commit himself on the coal issue without first consulting with the Americans, with whom the British were closely coordinating on Germany, particularly as a result of the merger of their two zones, which took effect on January 1, 1947.[10] Nevertheless, the British prime minister sent a note of warm regards to Blum on January 4, 1947. Following a second letter from Attlee on January 7, in which the latter evoked positively the idea of a visit by Blum to London (though still not committing himself on coal deliveries), the pace of events picked up. The French prime minister, acting in close coordination with his long-time friend and fellow Socialist, Vincent Auriol, who was about to be inaugurated as president, visited London on January 14 and 15, 1947.

Blum found in Foreign Secretary Ernest Bevin, who led the talks on the British side, a receptive interlocutor disposed to move speedily. Blum returned to Paris on the eve of his departure from the prime ministership with an agreement in principle for a British-French treaty of alliance. The essential step had thus been accomplished before the inauguration of Auriol as president of the Fourth Republic on January 16, 1947.

The French wanted to conclude this treaty with the British if possible before the impending opening of the conference of foreign ministers of the USSR, the United States, Britain, and France in Moscow, concerning a peace treaty with Germany. The French bureaucracy, always apt at taking the lead in international meetings, acted on the premise that, with a bilateral pact with the British in hand, the two countries would better coordinate their actions at the Big Four meeting. Therefore, the peace treaty would be less liable to contain provisions not in accord with the aims of French policy.[11]

After several weeks of polishing, the bilateral Anglo-French treaty was ready, and it was at that time that Foreign Minister Georges Bidault had the rather bizarre idea that the treaty be signed at Dunkirk—the place that had marked the end of the French-British military cooperation established in the 1930s. In his memoirs, Bidault claimed credit for this idea of Dunkirk as the venue:

At first sight, it was paradoxical and could appear a little provocative to choose . . . the place where, in the swirl of defeat . . . the French and the British competed over whose troops should get evacuated first. It was precisely to exorcise the poignant memory of the common defeat and the tragic confrontation that I wanted to renew the link at the place where it had been broken.[12]

The inexpugnable "tragic confrontation" at Dunkirk was such that, aboard the British evacuation fleet, the British went first and the French went last, which meant that not all the French made it. Some were casualties, some were made prisoners.[13]

On the other hand, perhaps the Treaty of Dunkirk was also, and particularly for pro-British figures such as Léon Blum and René Massigli, the French ambassador in London, a way of exorcising the cavalier way in which General de Gaulle decided at the end of the war to renew the ancient alliance with Russia rather than establish permanent links with his sponsors of 1940. In any event, just as the memory of Dunkirk was painful, so the memory of the Dunkirk Pact was not long-lasting. The renewal of the bilateral "Entente Cordiale" was to last just one year, to be replaced by a broader West European coalition in early 1948 and, in the following year by the Atlantic Alliance.

For France, the Dunkirk Pact, a mutual assistance treaty between Paris and London, and directed against Germany, was more or less the counterpart of the French-Soviet Treaty of December 1944, also directed against Germany. In fact, the Dunkirk Pact mentioned the treaties that each of the two allies had signed with the Soviet Union.[14] In view of this, the Dunkirk Treaty could not be expected to have any effect on French-

Soviet relations, although the Russians, as noted by their ambassador in
Paris, A. E. Bogomolov, would have preferred that the matter have been
handled in another manner. He told President Auriol that instead of a
bilateral treaty between Britain and France, it would have been better to
have a tripartite pact with the Soviet Union, an idea which Stalin had
accepted.[15]

In the long road that led from the Victory to NATO, the Treaty of
Dunkirk did not constitute a real turning point. In symbolic terms, the
treaty only served to complete the Victory: The three European members
of the grand alliance against Germany had each promised bilaterally to
act in such a way that Germany would never be able to threaten them
again.

In fact, the Treaty of Dunkirk was essentially an empty shell. Unlike
the other Western pacts that succeeded it, namely those of Brussels and
Washington, it had no follow-up in the sense of structures to complete the
agreement. The only innovation contained in the Treaty of Dunkirk was
the so-called automatic response provision by which Britain and France
committed themselves as follows: In the event of an attack by Germany
against either of the parties, the other party "will at once give the . . . party
so involved in hostilities all the military and other support and assistance
in his power."[16]

But the principle of "automatic response" in case of attack (Article II)
was somewhat watered down by what would take place in the phase prior
to the attack, that is, in the threat phase (Article I):

In the event of any threat to the security of either of [the parties] arising from the
adoption by Germany of a policy of aggression or from action by Germany de-
signed to facilitate such a policy, [the Parties will] take, after consulting with each
other and where appropriate with the other Powers having responsibility for action
in relation to Germany, such agreed action . . . as is best calculated to put an end
to this threat.[17]

The "other Powers having responsibility for action in relation to Germany" included, of course, the Soviet Union.

In view of the history between Britain and France since the Entente
Cordiale in 1903, it was highly unlikely that the two countries would not
find themselves on the same side in the event of a German attack. Moreover, such an attack, in 1947, was completely implausible. Nevertheless,
with the provision for "automatic response" in the event of an attack, an
important precedent had been created that could be applied a year later,
in the Brussels Pact, in a different context and at a moment when the Cold
War was intensifying in alarming proportions.

The import of the Treaty of Dunkirk was also somewhat vitiated by a
phrase in Article I, which stated that the accord was "without prejudice

to any . . . Treaty concluded between all the powers having responsibility for action in relation to Germany under Article 107 of the Charter of the United Nations."[18] (This phrase was in anticipation of the negotiations on Germany that were to begin six days later, on March 10, 1947, in Moscow, among the Big Four foreign ministers.) Furthermore, the mention in the Dunkirk Pact of the previous French-Soviet and Anglo-Soviet treaties meant implicitly that the two contracting parties of the pact would not act against Soviet interests.

Thus, at a moment when difficulties between the West and the Russians were increasing—and not long after Winston Churchill, in a speech at Zurich on October 19, 1946, had called for a reconciliation between France and Germany and the creation of a United States of Europe—the Treaty of Dunkirk, which was largely at French initiative, served only to reaffirm the links of the Entente Cordiale by raising the specter of a threatening Germany! It was therefore not surprising that, following a debate on the treaty in the Council of Ministers, President Auriol noted—perhaps with unselfconscious irony—that the treaty "was directed against no one."[19] In London, René Massigli observed from his post as ambassador, "The conclusion of the Treaty was not such as to retain for long the attention of British public opinion."[20]

What seems to have been particularly disappointing to the French officials who were pushing the Dunkirk Pact was the lukewarm attitude of London about a deeper commitment to the Continent in general and a willingness to give economic aid to France in particular. According to the final text, the two parties agreed simply that they would "by constant consultation on matters affecting their economic relations with each other take all possible steps to promote the prosperity and economic security of both countries."[21]

In fact, the Treaty of Dunkirk was rapidly overtaken de facto, because Germany had ceased to be an enemy, while the predecessor pact—the Treaty of Moscow—was also overtaken by the fact that the Soviet Union was no longer an ally.

DEGRADATION OF EAST-WEST RELATIONS

On March 6, 1947, two days after the signing of the Treaty of Dunkirk, President Vincent Auriol was chided by Gen. George C. Marshall, on a visit to Paris as secretary of state, for the uncoordinated action that had been taken with the British:

We believe that security lies in a treaty signed by the four major powers. Any regional agreement such as the one which has been signed recently at Dunkirk must, we believe, come within the framework of a wider security. It is this basic security that a treaty between the four powers could insure. . . . Rather than separate proposals, it would be desirable to have such a document define the control clauses over German war potential and establish the broad principles of disarmament and demilitarization.[22]

Marshall's desire for a common four-power position on Germany was to prove vain.

Since December 1944 and the signing of the French-Soviet treaty by de Gaulle, France had envisioned itself playing the role of intermediary between East and West. Georges Bidault, minister of Foreign Affairs from November 1944 onwards, and who had been present in this capacity for the signing of the French-Soviet Treaty in Moscow, followed in this line after the departure of de Gaulle at the beginning of 1946.[23]

However, French-Soviet relations had gone steadily downhill since the departure of de Gaulle. The year 1947 witnessed the beginning of the end of France's policy of nonalignment between East and West. The main aim of this policy, the securing of a privileged French position in Germany, was clearly not being met. Under the impulsion of its Christian Democratic (MRP) members, including Bidault, the French government began to move toward a policy of considering the USSR as the primary threat to the peace of Europe. According to Heike Bungert,

By early 1947, most French politicians had already given up the hope of obtaining the separation of the Rhineland and the Ruhr area from Germany and recognized the necessity for weakened France to join the Western camp once the CFM [Council of Foreign Ministers] had demonstrated to the French public that agreement with the Soviet Union was not possible.[24]

The Moscow conference of the Council of Foreign Ministers (CFM) of the Big Four, which began on March 10, 1947, six days after the signature of the Treaty of Dunkirk, ended in failure on April 24. It was a turning point, not only in the relations between the Anglo-Americans and the Soviets, but also in the bilateral relationship between France and the USSR. At Moscow, the French-Soviet rupture came from the Soviet side: Minister of Foreign Affairs Molotov refused to endorse the change of status of the Saar within the French zone of occupation and its attachment economically to France—an action that had been undertaken unilaterally by Paris in December 1946. Thus, while France's designs over the Ruhr and the Rhineland remained unfulfilled, its hold over the Saar became more problematic because of Soviet disapproval of French attempts to detach that region from Germany.

France's turn toward the West did not, however, mean the abandonment of its postwar policy of "keeping Germany down."[25] The contradiction between these two policies would become more acute as the cold war intensified.

During the spring of 1947, the climate of East-West relations began to deteriorate sharply. Communist parties were ejected from coalition governments in France, Italy, and Belgium. The Communist rebellion in Greece, which had been germinating since 1946, led President Harry Truman to ask the U.S. Congress for a special appropriation to combat it. This request was detailed in his speech of March 12, 1947, in which he asked for aid for Greece and for Turkey, also threatened by the Soviets. What was to become known as the "Truman Doctrine" speech marked the beginning of a profound change in U.S. strategic policy. It was the first step in what would eventually become a peacetime commitment to defend Europe in case of attack. That the U.S. commitment would extend even more broadly to areas outside Europe was also implicit in Truman's March 1947 speech, in the following sweeping passage: "I believe that it must be the policy of the United States to support free peoples who are resisting attempted subjugation by armed minorities or by outside pressures.[26]

The mechanism of response to the Soviet threat was being set in motion. Deputy Secretary of State Dean Acheson, not limiting himself to the most militarily threatened states of Greece and Turkey, directed on March 5, 1947, that there be undertaken urgently a study of "situations elsewhere in the world which may require analogous financial, technical and military aid on our part."[27]

Acheson's study led to the Marshall Plan, announced in a speech by the secretary of state at Harvard University on June 5, 1947. Following the advice of George Kennan, the chief of the State Department's Policy Planning Staff, the approach was a positive one: the economic recovery of Europe.[28] It was up to the Europeans to come up with proposals for aid required. The Soviets and the other Eastern European countries were also invited to join, and a conference at Paris was convened with their representatives in attendance. But shortly thereafter, on July 2, 1947, Soviet Foreign Minister Molotov announced that the USSR would not take part in the Marshall Plan, and the East Europeans were obliged to follow suit. The British and French foreign ministers, Ernest Bevin and Georges Bidault, then assumed the lead in the deliberations.

By autumn of 1947, events had evolved further. In Paris, the Communists, to their surprise, were still out of the government. From September 22 to 27, representatives of nine Communist parties met secretly in Szlarska Poreba, Poland, at which time a new international organization, the Cominform, was created. Although Stalin had officially disbanded the earlier Comintern in 1943, as a gesture to the Allies, the new organization was not simply a re-creation of the old one. Unlike the Comintern, the Cominform was limited to Europe, and its creation was a response to the threat of the Marshall Plan.[29]

At the meeting in Poland, Georgy Zhdanov, the newly named chairman, scolded the French and Italian Communist leaders present for having tried

to work in government coalitions with "bourgeois" parties. It was the end
of the Soviet experience in supporting such "Popular Front," or Left-
coalition, governments in Western Europe.

With the continuing forced absence of the French Communists from the
Socialist-led coalition government since May, it was only a matter of time
before Moscow would end the "Popular Front" line and return to an
attack on the "close enemy"—the European Socialists. The rupture with
the Socialists was made official in the declaration issued following the
formation of the Cominform, in which Léon Blum, Paul Ramadier, Clement Attlee, and Ernest Bevin were denounced as "right-wing socialists"
who were "behaving like traitors" in leading their countries into a "state
of dependent vassalage toward the United States."[30]

The creation of the Cominform was the signal for the Communists to
turn their agitation and propaganda (agit-prop) assets against the "bourgeois" governments of Western Europe, particularly those with large
Communist parties: France and Italy. Beginning in October, and lasting
into December, the Communists incited and led a series of insurrectional
strikes in France that eventually ran out of steam due to the vigorous
actions of the government of Paul Ramadier in the person of the interior
minister, Jules Moch.

FRENCH-AMERICAN MILITARY TALKS

In the middle of this period of sharp degradation in East-West relations
in late 1947, there began an official French initiative for military discussions with the United States. In the center of this approach was a military
officer who had a foot in the camps of both the Gaullists and the Christian
Democrats (the Mouvement Républicain Populaire [MRP]): General
Pierre Billotte, who at a certain point during the war had been de Gaulle's
chief of staff in London. Billotte had the double distinction of enjoying
the confidence of de Gaulle and of the foreign minister, Georges Bidault,
and he regretted that an incompatibility developed between the two: "It
was unfortunate that Bidault clashed with de Gaulle and the two men
became separated politically," he wrote.[31] Billotte retained his loyalty to
de Gaulle after the latter's departure from power but also remained close
to Bidault, who stayed on as foreign minister. He was thus an acceptable
figure to the Gaullist movement and the MRP, who, though on opposite
sides of the political fence, can be said also to have been "objective allies"
in their antipathy toward the French Communist Party.

At the moment that de Gaulle left the government in January 1946,
Billotte held the post of deputy chief of staff of the Army. He was one of
a number of Gaullists in civil and military positions who remained in the
French administration after the general's departure. In the temporary absence in London of his chief, General Alphonse Juin, Billotte, as acting

chief of the Army, played a role in the formation of the new government. He exerted his influence with Maurice Schumann (a former Gaullist), so that the latter's party, the MRP, would enter into a coalition government with the Socialists and the Communists. If the MRP had not entered this so-called tripartite coalition, a Communist, Maurice Thorez, could instead have become prime minister of a Communist-Socialist coalition government.[32]

Shortly thereafter, Billotte was assigned to New York as French representative to the Military Staff Committee of the United Nations. This committee had begun meeting in London on February 4, 1946,[33] but then moved on to UN Headquarters at Lake Success, New York. Billotte took over from Gen. Martial Valin as head of the French military mission to the United Nations and participated in his first meeting with this committee, composed of military representatives of the five permanent members of the Security Council, on March 26.[34]

Billotte had been assigned as the Army delegate (and therefore the chief) of the French Military Mission to the United Nations by Minister of the Armies Edmond Michelet, who was a Gaullist appointed to the post on November 21, 1945.[35] It was Michelet who was in charge of making this appointment. Michelet gave Billotte a general brief to engage in exploratory talks with American military authorities.[36]

Billotte's assignment had the approval of both General de Gaulle and of Billotte's superior, General Juin, although the mission had become watered down from a more official one originally envisaged by Billotte with de Gaulle—what Billotte in his memoir described as discussions with the Americans leading to an "Atlantic" pact.[37] What put a stop to the original mission has been described variously by Billotte in his own memoir and by the historian Georgette Elgey. According to Billotte, he briefed the new president of the provisional government, Félix Gouin, who took office on January 26, 1946, and the latter proceeded to brief the new vice president of the Council of Ministers, the Communist Maurice Thorez.[38] This effectively put an end to the original mission.

According to Elgey, it was through a leak on the American side that Billotte's mission, which had been approved by Bidault as foreign minister, became known to the French ambassador in Washington, Henri Bonnet. The latter reported the matter to Paris, and Gouin, who had not been informed, put a stop to it.[39]

The initiation of secret military talks per se with the United States had to wait until the Socialists relinquished the prime ministership in autumn of 1947. On the political level, the lead was taken by Bidault, the perpetual minister of Foreign Affairs, and by the new prime minister, Robert Schuman, whose nomination was approved by the National Assembly on November 22, in the midst of a series of insurrectional strikes led by the Communists.[40]

As soon as the new Schuman government was in place, Billotte, by his own account, wrote a personal letter to the prime minister, suggesting that secret military discussions be held between the French and the Americans on the subject of France's security.[41] Billotte's propositions were aimed in particular at persuading the Americans to accept the idea that the defense of Western Europe take place as far to the east of France as possible, rather than concentrating on a peripheral line of defense, running in an arc from North Africa through the Pyrenees to Great Britain.[42] It was a debate that was to continue in parallel in the United States, France, and Britain. In the United States, it went on for two years before the strategy of "forward defense" advocated by the Army and the Navy against the "peripheral" thesis of the Air Force was accepted definitively.[43]

In France, the two rival theses were also at work within the French defense hierarchy, as pointed out by Georges-Henri Soutou.[44] The chief proponent of "forward defense" in France was Gen. Jean de Lattre de Tassigny,[45] who on November 30, 1945, had been named inspector general of the French Armed Forces as well as president of the Supreme War Council. The latter position meant that he would become in wartime the commander of the French Armed Forces.[46] In a reorganization announced on March 11, 1947, however, de Lattre retained the sole function of inspector general of the Army, while Gen. Georges Revers became chief of the General Staff of the Army.[47]

It was de Lattre along with Gen. Alphonse Juin who had been the leading figures in the command of the French North African Army, which had fought in Italy and in the invasion of Southern France. Juin, who had been named chief of the General Staff of National Defense in August 1944 under the provisional government of Charles de Gaulle, was appointed resident general of France in Morocco in May 1947 with the concurrent title of commander-in-chief of the North African Theater of Operations.[48]

In a larger, political context, de Lattre and Juin were on opposite sides of what Soutou described as a "fundamental divergence of orientation, however muffled, within the French political and military world."[49] There were those, chiefly de Lattre and President Auriol, who favored building up a strong European bloc based on France, the United Kingdom and the Benelux countries, to which the United States would provide military support. In this way, the European or Western bloc ("Bloc occidental") would retain its own cohesion and not become a simple military appendage of the United States.

Another group, which opposed this thesis, and which was represented by Bidault, Juin, and Billotte,[50] felt that it tied France's future too closely with that of Great Britain. If the two countries were politically and militarily bound up with each other, this inexorably led to the former, as an "Anglo-Saxon" power, assuming the role of "screen" or intermediary between the United States and France. Juin and Billotte preferred to have France negotiate directly with the United States, as by far the most powerful potential ally, and to draw up defense arrangements bilaterally with Washington.

Each of these groups had a different way of looking at the preservation of national independence, the sine qua non of all French policy in the postwar period, given the disaster of 1940. Among the Socialists, Vincent Auriol and Paul Ramadier, in particular, sought to preserve the integrity of the European or Western bloc as a means of strengthening the personality and status of Europe and the French role in it. In this attitude, they merged with the more liberal (in the European sense) current represented by Jean Monnet and Robert Schuman, both of whom saw the construction of a unified Europe as a way out of France's postwar problems.

Though the political appreciation of the situation intersected with the military appreciation, there was not a total congruence of approach: While de Lattre was the leading proponent of "forward defense," most French officers could see the benefit of this approach, as it meant that France would be relatively more important because its army would be brought into play from the outset of hostilities with the USSR.

Those who advocated what was later to become known as a European defense identity tended also to be neutralist in political outlook. The argument of the neutralist group was that such a policy was necessary to preserve social peace in a politically polarized France, and that it was also a prudent policy that was less liable to provoke the Soviets into launching hostilities.

The neutralist group was mainly represented by President Auriol and Prime Minister Ramadier on the civilian side and by de Lattre on the military side. De Lattre was a regular contact of Auriol, as seen through the latter's journal. In 1946, when the prevailing current was still that of a France "between East and West," Gen. Paul Ely, chief of the Military Cabinet of the Minister of the Armies, recommended in a note of August 23 that France should enter the war on the side of whichever of the two blocs, East or West that was first attacked.[51]

On June 3, 1947, even after the ouster of the Communists by the Ramadier government, de Lattre and Auriol agreed that France should keep all its options open in the event of a war between the United States and the USSR. France's policy should be either that of "neutrality, or entry into the war on one or the other side."[52]

By the middle of 1947, however, this French form of neutralism was not a widely shared sentiment within the government, not to speak of within the military. On September 23, 1947, a paper submitted by General Jean Humbert, who had become acting chief of the National Defense Staff after General Juin's departure for Morocco in May, was presented to a restricted meeting of the Cabinet. Humbert's paper argued that a policy of neutrality was impossible, and that for fundamental political reasons, France should align itself squarely with the "Anglo-Saxon" camp. To remain neutral would deprive France of U.S. aid and would mean that in the event of war with the Soviet Union, the French Empire would be seized by Anglo-American forces.[53]

According to Billotte, after he had sent his letter to Schuman advocating secret military talks with the United States, it was Bidault who took charge of the matter and raised it with General Marshall in London in December 1947.[54] Marshall, delighted with this French initiative, gave his agreement and suggested that a British representative be included in these military talks.[55] Following this, and according to Bidault's papers, the latter conveyed to Marshall a text advocating the conclusion of a secret military agreement between France and the United States for the defense of Western Europe. This was done through Billotte on December 29, 1947.[56]

These bilateral French-American contacts were kept from the Socialist leadership, in particular the chief of state, Vincent Auriol, and his ex-prime minister, Paul Ramadier, who was later to return as minister of National Defense.[57] According to Billotte's account,

It was Bidault who, at the end of 1947, followed up on my request. He immediately took responsibility for launching the Atlantic affair with Marshall and Truman and assigned the negotiations to me. Well aware of the weaknesses of judgment of the President of the Republic and of [Paul Ramadier] . . . he was careful not to put them in the picture during this preliminary phase and asked me to remain likewise silent about it.[58]

According to American files, General Marshall suggested to General Eisenhower, who was then chief of staff of the Army, that he put a senior officer in contact with Billotte.[59] This presumably took place as a result of Bidault's letter to Marshall, delivered on December 29, 1947. Eisenhower responded by naming as Billotte's contact Gen. Matthew Ridgway, at that time the American counterpart of Billotte on the Military Staff Committee of the United Nations.

In accordance with Marshall's suggestion, a British participant was added to the arrangement. This was Gen. Frederick Morgan, also a member of the Military Staff Committee of the United Nations as were Billotte and Ridgway. The first of a series of military talks on collective defense in Europe among these three representatives took place at a fort near New York City in January 1948.[60] These military talks were to take place at times in a trilateral mode but most often in a bilateral (French-American) one, which was the most fruitful from the point of view of the French.

There seems to be no official U.S. record of French-American conversations dealing in specific terms with the mandate behind the talks with

Billotte. However, if it had been agreed to launch secret military talks, it would be understandable, especially at the beginning, not to commit anything to writing.

The launching of military talks between France and the United States in late 1947 took place against a background of widespread social unrest in France, incited by the Communist Party.[61] General Marshall, as the man who sanctioned these talks, had become gravely preoccupied by what he called "the critical state of affairs in France" in which he saw "a very real struggle for power" going on. In Marshall's view, there would be a "far-reaching significance to Germany, Italy, the Mediterranean, North Africa, and to other areas, were France to fall."[62]

"The dogs bark, the caravan passes," as General de Gaulle was fond of repeating: the revolutionary wave in France subsided. A split within the trade union movement developed. Some Socialists, concerned that the Communists were trying to achieve a breakdown of society, broke away from the Communist-dominated Confederation générale du travail and formed a rival organization called Force Ouvrière. The government held firm and even ordered a call-up of draftees to help maintain public order.

In Washington, the bill for interim aid until the Marshall Plan could take effect on April 1, 1948, was passed by the U.S. House of Representatives on December 17, 1947, and helped to calm the economic crisis in France and Italy during the winter of 1947–1948. With the passage of the interim aid bill and the advent of The Marshall Plan the following spring, France passed definitively into the Western camp. The chance of a Communist regime coming into power in France had gone away.

NOTES

1. François Mitterrand, *De l'Allemagne, de la France* (Paris: Odile Jacob, 1996), 43.

2. Pierre Lassalle, "Sécurité face à l'Est dans l'immédiat après-guerre," in *De Gaulle et la Nation face aux problèmes de défense*, Colloquium organized by the Institut d'histoire du temps présent and the Institut Charles-de-Gaulle, October 21–22, 1982 (Paris: Plon, 1983), 118.

3. Alain Peyrefitte, *C'était de Gaulle* (Paris: Fayard, 1994), 153.

4. Georges-Henri Soutou, "La securité de la France dans l'après-guerre," in *La France et l'OTAN, 1949–1996*, ed. Maurice Vaïsse, Pierre Mélandri, and Frédéric Bozo (Brussels: Éditions Complexe, 1996), 24.

5. As of December 31, 1946, the French Army totaled 400,000, the Air Force 50,000, and the Navy 45,000. (*Informations Militaires* no. 46 [1946]: 6). By 1950, the French armed forces had increased to 658,000, and of this number 150,000 were fighting in Indochina. (*Ibid.*, 1950, no. 160, 4).

6. Cooper had earlier been British representative to the French Committee of National Liberation in Algiers.

7. René Massigli, *Une comédie des erreurs* (Paris: Plon, 1978), 87–88.

8. Ibid., 87.

9. Ibid., 89.

10. The so-called Bizonal Agreement merging the British and American occupation zones in Germany had been signed on December 2, 1946, in New York between British Foreign Secretary Ernest Bevin and U.S. Secretary of State James Byrnes.

11. Massigli, *Une comédie des erreurs*, 89–90. N.B. For a statement of the aims of French policy toward Germany, see p. 42.

12. Georges Bidault, *D'une résistance à l'autre* (Paris: Les Presses du Siècle, 1965), 145. It should be added, however, that according to the journal of Vincent Auriol, the main factor behind the choice of venue was that Ernest Bevin should not be asked to come to Paris because the British minister of foreign affairs was unwell at that moment (Vincent Auriol, *Journal du septennat* (Paris: Armand Colin, 1974), 1: 106).

13. See also Introduction, p. xi.

14. In the preamble is the following mention: "Having regard to the Treaties of Alliance and Mutual Assistance which they have respectively concluded with the Union of Soviet Socialist Republics" (Great Britain, Parliament, *Parliamentary Papers*, 1947–1948, Treaty Series No. 73 [1947], Cmd, 7217, 2).

15. Auriol, *Journal du septennat*, 1: 123.

16. Great Britain, Parliament, *Parliamentary Papers*, 1947–1948, Cmd. 7217, 4.

17. Ibid.

18. Ibid. Article 107 is as follows: "Nothing in the present Charter shall invalidate or preclude action, in relation to any state which during the Second World War has been an enemy of any signatory to the present Charter, taken or authorized as a result of that war by the Governments having the responsibility for such action." The purpose of Article 107 was to make it clear that the making of the peace following World War II would proceed as independently of the U.N. Charter as if that document did not exist (*Charter of the United Nations: Commentary and Documents*, ed. Leland M. Goodrich, Edvard Hambro, and Anne P. Simons [New York: Columbia University Press, 1969], 633).

19. Auriol, *Journal du septennat*, 1: 199. (Entry of March 4, 1947.)

20. Massigli, *Une comédie des erreurs*, 92.

21. Great Britain, Parliament, *Parliamentary Papers*, 1947–1948, Cmd. 7217, 4.

22. *Foreign Relations of the United States* (FRUS) (1947), vol. 2, *Council of Foreign Ministers; Germany and Austria* (Washington, D.C.: Government Printing Office, 1992), 194.

23. Alfred Grosser, *The Western Alliance* (New York: Continuum, 1980), 60.

24. Heike Bungert, "A New Perspective on French-American Relations during the Occupation of Germany, 1945–1948: Behind-the-Scenes Diplomatic Bargaining and the Zonal Merger," *Diplomatic History* 18, 3 (summer 1994): 346.

25. Lord Lionel Ismay, secretary-general of NATO from 1952–1957, was the author of the famous formula that the purpose of that organization was to keep the Americans "in," the Soviets "out," and the Germans "down."

26. Dean Acheson, *Present at the Creation: My Years in the State Department* (New York: W. W. Norton, 1969), 222.

27. FRUS (1947), Vol. 3, *The British Commonwealth; Europe* (1972), 197.

28. Ibid., 224–25.

29. Scott D. Parrish, "The Turn Toward Confrontation: The Soviet Reaction to the Marshall Plan, 1947," in "New Evidence on the Soviet Rejection of the Marshall Plan: Two Reports," *Cold War International History Project* (Washington, D.C.: Woodrow Wilson Center, 1995), 32 n. 83.

30. *Le Monde*, October 7, 1947, 3.

31. Pierre Billotte, *Le passé au futur* (Paris: Stock, 1979), 50.

32. Pierre Billotte, *Le temps des armes* (Paris: Plon, 1972), 418–23.

33. *Informations Militaires* no. 45 (1946): 7.

34. Billotte, *Le passé au futur*, 17.

35. This was the date that this ministry was created (*Informations Militaires* no. 46 [1946]: 6). It took the place of the Ministry of National Defense.

36. Billotte, *Le temps des armes*, 435–36.

37. Ibid., 423.

38. Ibid., 429.

39. Georgette Elgey, *La République des illusions* (Paris: Fayard, 1965), 1: 118.

40. See also p. 26, this chapter.

41. Billotte, *Le passé au futur*, 41.

42. Ibid., 44–46.

43. Thomas M. Sisk, "Forging the Weapon: Eisenhower as NATO's Supreme Commander, Europe, 1950–1952," in *Eisenhower: A Centenary Assessment*, ed. Gunter Bischof and Stephen E. Ambrose (Baton Rouge: Louisiana State University Press, 1995), 67.

44. Soutou, "La sécurité de la France dans l'après-guerre," 33–35.

45. Ibid., 35.

46. Jean de Lattre, *Ne pas subir: Écrits, 1914–1952* (Paris: Plon, 1984), 332.

47. *Informations Militaires* no. 91 (1947): 1.

48. Ibid., 1950, no. 146, 7.

49. Soutou, "La sécurité de la France dans l'après-guerre," 35.

50. Ibid.

51. Ibid., 27.

52. Auriol, *Journal du septennat*, vol. 1 (1947), 253.

53. Soutou, "La sécurité de la France dans l'après-guerre," 32. According to Young, *France, the Cold War and the Western Alliance* (Leicester, U.K.: Leicester University Press, 1990), pp. 170–72, an EMGDN memorandum aimed at the abandonment of France's neutrality policy was presented to Ramadier on October 27. Though there is a discrepancy in the date, it is possible that more than one EMGDN paper making such a recommendation was presented to Ramadier.

54. There was indeed a meeting between Bidault and Marshall on December 17, 1947, in London. According to the American account of this meeting, it was focused exclusively on the German problem. There is nothing in it on Billotte. However, if there were discussions on the latter's mission, it may have been decided not to mention this in the official account, which is contained in FRUS (1947), 2: 813–15.

55. Ibid. According to the account of Georgette Elgey, Bidault, who was being pressed by Billotte, suggested to General Marshall in October 1947 that there be an American commitment to the defense of Europe; this was during a side meeting between the two at the time of the annual session of the UN General Assembly in New York (*La République des illusions*, 1: 380). However, there is no indication

of this in the American report of the meeting of October 8, 1947 between Bidault and Marshall in New York—the only meeting that was held between the two during that month. It appears from this account that the meeting dealt exclusively with the Ruhr (FRUS [1947], 2: 683–85). This meeting had been preceded by another meeting between the two men on September 18, 1947, also in New York, at which time, again according to the American account, Bidault said to Marshall that he wanted to undertake a high-level dialogue with the United States on all aspects concerning Germany. Bidault hoped that these discussions could take place within the following days, during the course of his stay in the United States (Ibid., p. 680). Marshall replied politely that he was a little bit out of the circuit, as he had just returned from a meeting in Rio de Janeiro, where a security pact among the American states had been signed. First of all, said Marshall, the German problem should be studied more profoundly; also, it would probably be necessary to associate the British as well with such talks (Ibid., 681). There was no immediate sequel to this exchange, except that at their next meeting, on October 8, Bidault made reference to informal talks on the Ruhr which had been held in New York. There is nothing on these talks in the record (Ibid., 680).

56. Soutou, "La sécurité de la France dans l'après-guerre," 34. According to Billotte's memoir, Bidault made a visit to him at his home in Connecticut in December 1947 for the purpose of confirming to him this new mission of contact with the Americans (Billotte, *Le passé au futur*, 58). Billotte also recounted that he took Bidault's text to Marshall on December 29, 1947 (Ibid., 59).

57. Billotte, *Le passé au futur*, 50.

58. Ibid.

59. FRUS (1949), 4, *Western Europe* (1975), 294. On February 7, 1948, Eisenhower left his position as chief of staff of the Army and was replaced by Gen. Omar N. Bradley. Eisenhower then became president of Columbia University.

60. Elgey, *La République des illusions*, 1: 381.

61. See pp. 26–27, this chapter.

62. FRUS (1947), 3: 808. (Telegram from London on December 2, 1947, asking that Congress be urged to pass an interim aid bill, which would tide France over until the Marshall Plan went into effect on April 1, 1948.)

CHAPTER 3

The Turn toward Europe: The Brussels Treaty and the Western Union

We looked for a hero-symbol, and we had one without knowing it. We sensed that what was lacking in Pétain, it was that, that unshakeable unity, that faith in the life of a people less sensitive to constancy than to courage. That was the force of de Gaulle.

François Mitterrand on the French and the French Resistance[1]

That a people without form, such as that of Germany, could seize and absorb [France] like a blister seemed to me blasphemous. What were all these people doing in my country? Their accent irritated me more than their tanks. This way of commanding, of ordering around the oldest nation in the world, they who didn't have two centuries behind them.

François Mitterrand on the Germans and the German Occupation[2]

THE TREATY OF BRUSSELS

The combination of the meaninglessness of The Treaty of Dunkirk, a pact aimed at a prostrate Germany, and the rising tide of Soviet influence in eastern and central Europe, led the nations of Western Europe to come together out of necessity. Thus was born the Brussels Pact, in early 1948.

The Treaty of Brussels, one year after that of Dunkirk, was of a totally different nature, although at the beginning it was conceived simply to extend the preceding treaty to the Benelux countries. The inspiration behind the Treaty of Brussels, signed on March 17, 1948, came from British Minister of Foreign Affairs Ernest Bevin. Bevin had launched his initiative in the aftermath of the "conference of the last chance"—the meeting of the Big Four foreign ministers in London—in December 1947, which represented one more attempt to arrive at an agreement on a peace treaty with Germany (and Austria). It ended in failure in the middle of that month. It was obvious that a dead end had been reached in the U.S. policy aim of a quadripartite treaty on Germany (France, Britain, United States, USSR), as had been proposed by the former secretary of state James Byrnes in a speech at Stuttgart on September 6, 1946.[3]

At the end of the London conference, General Marshall held separate meetings there with his counterparts, Georges Bidault and Ernest Bevin. The object of these meetings was to examine future options, in view of the failure of the Big Four to come to an agreement.

According to American records, the meeting with Bidault, on December 17, was confined to Germany;[4] by contrast, in the talks with Bevin on December 17 and 18, the latter proposed to Marshall "a sort of spiritual federation of the West."[5] If one could build a powerful combination in the West, said Bevin, the Soviet Union would realize that, having progressed up to a certain point, it could go no farther.[6]

Bevin told Marshall he was now thinking in terms of a treaty including, besides Britain and France, the Benelux countries and Italy. What was important, said Bevin, was to impart a sense of confidence to the Western Europeans and to convince them that the encroachments of the Communists were definitely going to be stopped.[7]

Bevin maintained to Marshall that the problem of the security of Europe concerned France even more than Britain. In this regard, he considered that the spiritual consolidation of Western civilization was now possible, and when this was accomplished, France could return again as a great power. Bevin asked for (and presumably received) authorization from Marshall to create an official Anglo-French committee to discuss the whole gamut of problems in the area of security.

But at the same time, Bevin suggested that there be Anglo-American discussions on security such as had been held shortly before on the Middle East.[8] The British tactic seemed to be twofold: first, that a British "screen" be maintained between the French and the Americans; second, that the French be kept at a level below that of the British.

Several days later, on December 22, 1947, in a message from London to Washington, Bevin asked Marshall's permission to convey to Bidault the essence of what had been discussed in the meetings between the American secretary of state and himself. This would give Bidault the feeling that, as Bevin put it, he was a "member of the club"; moreover, Bidault had asked for a written account of these meetings.[9] The State Department agreed in a telegram two days later.[10]

Possibly spurred on by Bevin's account of his meeting with Marshall, and in any event always sensitive to being outshone by his British counterpart, Bidault then wrote to Marshall. This, as we have seen in the previous chapter,[11] was the letter that was delivered on December 29, 1947, by Billotte. In the letter, Bidault advocated a secret military agreement between France and the United States within the framework of a larger Western alliance.[12]

On January 13, 1948, the British ambassador in Washington, Lord Inverchapel, sent to Marshall a memorandum[13] containing Bevin's plan for a Western union, the conception of which, according to Bevin, had already been discussed with Bidault. Bevin envisaged the swift conclusion of a treaty with the Benelux countries—a treaty that would resemble the Treaty of Dunkirk. Such a proposal would be subject to Bidault's agreement. Inverchapel's note transmitting Bevin's memorandum stated in part:

You will recall that, after the breakdown of the Council of Foreign Ministers in London [in December], Mr. Bevin gave you an outline of his proposals for a Western Union. He has since given further thought to this important problem and has embodied his ideas in a paper, of which he has asked me to give you very secretly the attached summary.

As the first step toward the realization of this wide project, Mr. Bevin is suggesting to M. Bidault forthwith that the British and French Governments should make a joint offer of a treaty to Belgium, Holland and Luxembourg. If M. Bidault agrees, Mr. Bevin proposes that they should at once concert a draft treaty which should, in Mr. Bevin's view, follow the lines of the Treaty of Dunkirk.

After having created a hard core in Western Europe, the British ambassador's note continued, it would then be necessary to find the best means to extend the system that Bevin had conceived; that is, to associate other states with it, including Italy, other states of the Mediterranean, and the Scandinavian countries. In Bevin's memorandum, he also recommended that Spain and Germany eventually be included because without these countries such a system would not be complete.

Bevin also recalled that, in a general way, he had already broached his overall idea, which he termed a "spiritual union of the West" with Marshall and with Bidault, and that the reaction of both had been favorable. Bevin added that he was shortly going to speak on this subject before the House of Commons.

At this point, events began to move quickly. On January 21, the French and British ambassadors in the Benelux countries, in parallel démarches, suggested to the host governments discussions aimed at a treaty of alliance, which would be in effect an extension of the Treaty of Dunkirk. The following day, Bevin placed before the House of Commons the principal points of his plan for an alliance of these countries of Western Europe. Bevin's presentation, however, was more sweeping than French thinking on the subject. Paris had been informed of the timing of Bevin's announcement in the House of Commons but not of its content.

In his speech to the Commons on January 22, Bevin was intent on delivering several messages, not all of them consistent. On the one hand, he advocated an extension pure and simple of the Dunkirk Pact to the Benelux countries. On the other hand, he extended the notion of the threat beyond Germany to the Soviet Union, by referring to a statement he had made a year earlier, when he had been asked if the Dunkirk Pact might one day include Belgium. Bevin had replied yes, and he had added that the role of Great Britain was to prevent the outbreak of a new conflict in the West, *whether it came from Germany or elsewhere* (emphasis added).[14]

At the same time, and in the background of his basic proposition concerning the extension of the Dunkirk Pact to the Benelux countries, Bevin embellished his speech with a number of concepts both moral and vague, or as could be perceived as such by the French. After having deplored the return of the "police state" in Europe so quickly following the defeat of fascism, and after having listed Soviet actions aimed at "bringing about the failure of Western Europe or intimidating it by means of political agitation, economic chaos and even revolutionary methods,"[15] Bevin concluded:

All these developments which I have just mentioned leads us to the conclusion that the nations of Western Europe must close ranks. These countries have so much in common. Our sacrifices during the war, our hatred of injustice and oppression, our parliamentary democracy, our struggle for economic rights, and our idea and our love of liberty are common to us all.... I think that the time has come for a consolidation of Western Europe.[16]

As it was put by Jean Chauvel, secretary-general of the Quai d'Orsay and the person in charge of reconciling the French approach with the rhetoric of Bevin contained in the British text, the latter "was liable to appear as a Holy Alliance, with all that this concept suggested in terms of the negative reaction it would arouse in French public opinion."[17] However, Chauvel upon his arrival in London on March 3, 1948, was told in forceful terms by his British interlocutors that Bevin "had an essential interest in placing the [proposed] pact in the same context mentioned in his initial speech [in the Commons]."[18] It was important to Bevin, according to Chauvel's negotiating counterpart, Sir Orme Sargent,

to avoid, both for considerations of internal politics and parliamentary tactics, and also to take account of the wishes and imperatives of the American Government, that the [proposed] pact not appear as a document of a military nature and inspired by imperialist ambitions, but as an instrument of defense of a ... complex civilization which was evolving in its own different ways.[19]

The reference to the wishes of the American government may have had to do with the viewpoint of George Kennan, author of the concept of *containment* of the Soviet Union.[20] Kennan had expressed his reservations about the plan for a Western Union in a memorandum of January 20, 1948, of which the following are extracts:

- Military union should not be the starting point. It should flow from the political, economic and spiritual union—not vice versa.
- The introduction of the note of military defense right at the outset might frighten several of the outlying countries (notably the Scandinavians) rather than attract them.
- The role of the German people in any European union will eventually be of prime importance. The general adoption of a mutual assistance pact based squarely on defense against Germany is a poor way to prepare the ground for the eventual entry of the Germans into this concept.[21]

For France, the problem with this idea of spiritual union, which was so dear to Bevin, George Kennan, and others, was that France had been the first country in Europe to de-Christianize itself, so to speak. Spiritual references tended to produce a reflex of rejection in the secular and republican mindset of the French. Even political concepts, such as democracy, were perceived differently by the French than by the Anglo-Americans. François Furet has put his finger on this gulf of incomprehension, by observing that American civilization "is in its reality both too mixed in with the Christian faith and too confident about the idea of free enterprise to attract all those who cannot think of the future of democracy except as separated from Christianity and from capitalism: the innumerable children of the French Revolution."[22]

Moreover, in the eyes of the French, the United States was hardly an ideal countermodel to the Soviet Union—especially in this postwar climate, when the prestige of the Soviet Union as the principal conqueror of Nazi Germany was at its height, and when most French intellectuals, with the exception of Raymond Aron, Albert Camus, and a number of others, looked on the Soviet Union with a sympathetic eye. There was a virtuousness surrounding the image of the heroic Red Army struggling to overcome the Wehrmacht—a virtuousness enhanced by contrast with the fact that it was the Americans who had dropped the atomic bomb on Japan.

The French leadership, and especially the neutralist current represented by the chief of state, Vincent Auriol, hesitated to link together anticommunism and anti-Sovietism. Although locked in a struggle with an insurrectional communism in France, they continued to hope that the Soviet Union and the Western countries would find some way to reach an agreement, and the many references to this in Auriol's journal, which have a certain irenic quality, are a testimony to this.

The French leadership also had to take into account its own public

opinion, which was still under the influence of the reigning antifascism of
the era, an antifascism which, as François Furet observed, had a potent
appeal. It was a "negation which unified East and West"; it gave to the
recently ended war an overall meaning[23]; and it was, in its most radical
expression, anticapitalist.[24] The prevailing mind-set of the postwar period,
and particularly the case in France, was that fascism was basically a cap-
italist phenomenon. Quite to the contrary, as Furet has pointed out, fascism's ideological appeal rested on its rejection of capitalism:

Between Socialism and anti-liberal, even anti-democratic, thought, one can see
that the complicity goes way back. Since the French Revolution, the reactionary
Right and the Socialist Left shared the same denunciation of bourgeois individu-
alism, and the same conviction that modern society, deprived of real foundations,
and prisoner of the illusion of universal rights, does not have a solid future.[25]

On the other side of the Atlantic, enlightened figures such as George
Kennan, the leading diplomatic expert on the Soviet Union, could appreciate that the idea of military pacts had a hollow ring for the people of
Western Europe, who were still far from recovered from the effects of the
Second World War. Little by little, by way of filling a spiritual void, and
at the same time of providing a strategic and moral raison d'être for a
new engagement of the United States in Europe, a number of American
and European intellectuals seemed to take up the theme of the influential
journalist Walter Lippmann. Lippmann, in a book appearing in 1944 entitled *United States War Aims* (a sequel to his earlier *United States Foreign
Policy*), sketched a picture of cultural and historical affinities on both sides
of the Atlantic—what he described as an "Atlantic civilization."[26] In the
postwar period, a joint study was published on the same theme, by a
Frenchman, Jacques Godechot, and an American, Robert Palmer, with
the title of *The Problem of the Atlantic*.[27] In this study, the authors recognized Lippmann as the originator of this concept:

Lippmann was clearly the first to use the expression "Atlantic Community." For
him the Atlantic Community was a political and economic grouping, established
little by little by all the great powers bordering the ocean, strengthened by the
"Atlantic Charter," and destined to develop in the future, thanks to the good
neighbor principle and to the organization of increasingly active economic exchanges.[28]

In *United States War Aims* and other writings, Lippmann proposed a
series of "orbits" that would coexist peacefully after the war: an Atlantic
orbit, a Soviet orbit, and an eventual Chinese orbit.[29] Lippmann's view,
according to his biographer Ronald Steel was that "the 'primary aim' of
American responsibility was the basin of the Atlantic on both sides, and

the Pacific islands—in other words, the Atlantic community plus a 'blue-water' strategy of naval bases and roaming fleets. Outside these regions there should be no permanent military or political commitments."[30]

France's difficulty with this emphasis on Atlantic affinities, linking the Old World with the New, was that the Atlantic, as Jacques Godechot and Robert Palmer put it, had been dominated by England from the eighteenth century onwards[31] and that at the end of the nineteenth century this hegemony had been replaced by a combined American, British, and Canadian one.[32] Thus, the "Atlantic" world was a world in which France could never enjoy first place.

Moreover, the first significant embodiment of what was to become the institutionalization of the Atlantic idea was the Atlantic Charter, signed between Franklin Roosevelt and Winston Churchill on August 14, 1941, off the waters of Newfoundland. This sweeping declaration of war aims, as one American historian put it, "committed the two English-speaking powers to work for a postwar international order reminiscent of the one that Wilson had vainly attempted to forge a generation earlier."[33] On September 24, 1941, fifteen other signatories endorsed the charter, including the Free French. However, the latter were expressly excluded from the first anniversary celebration of the charter because of Franklin Roosevelt's pique at General de Gaulle's unilateral seizure of two Vichy-held islands in the North Atlantic, St. Pierre and Miquelon.

Thus, the term "Atlantic" has an unwelcome ring to French ears.

EFFECT OF THE PRAGUE COUP

In early 1948, the important thing from France's point of view was to obtain a security guarantee from the United States. George Bidault, who had already said to the American ambassador in London on December 17, 1947, that he feared President Edouard Benes would be ousted by the Communists in Czechoslovakia,[34] sounded a cry of alarm after the Prague coup two months later.

Czechoslovakia represented a special case in the Western mind. It had been abandoned in 1938–1939 by the West, and especially by France: Paris did not honor its bilateral treaty with Prague. A democracy since its creation by the Versailles Treaty in 1919, Czechsolvakia had a rich cultural tradition and long ties with the West. Though not a country of Western Europe, it was like a dagger into the heart of Europe: parts of it were more "western" in geography than Germany. Seen from the opposing side, as Czech Communist leader Rudolf Slansky had put it at the meeting creating the Cominform in September 1947, "Czechoslovakia is the westernmost bastion of new democracy."[35]

More than any other event in the postwar period, the Communist takeover in Czechoslovakia in February 1948 served as a political alarm signal to the West. The specter of Stalin "picking off" European countries one by one, as Hitler had done, was beginning to take hold in the Western consciousness.

On March 4, 1948, in the wake of the Communist coup in Prague, Bidault sent an urgent and lengthy letter to General Marshall. Recalling President Truman's declaration of March 12, 1947, in which the American president had called for a program of aid to Greece and Turkey and more generally, "a policy of aid to free peoples at present resisting maneuvers of . . . armed minorities and external pressures," Bidault noted that, since the president's speech, an entire "intermediate zone" in central and eastern Europe had fallen under Soviet domination: Hungary, Bulgaria, Rumania, Poland, and now Czechoslovakia. This meant that "at this point the borders of Soviet political influence coincide with the borders of its military power. . . . Everything must be done to prevent a repetition in Austria, in Italy or elsewhere of what has just taken place in Prague."[36]

France, continued Bidault, could not alone, nor even with the allies it was seeking to bring together (in the Brussels Pact) be able to hold out against the Soviets.[37] Consequently, Bidault proposed that three-way talks be held between the United States, Britain, and France to discuss urgently the problem of a common defense.[38]

Marshall replied on March 12, 1948, stating that it would be better to wait for the outcome of the discussions taking place at Brussels over the new pact, out of which were to emerge arrangements for a common defense. Such arrangements were a precondition for a larger defensive system in which the United States might take part. Marshall added in his reply that "as soon as my Government has had a chance to study the Brussels accords, I will be ready to discuss with you and Mr. Bevin the next steps to take. It probably would be desirable to include a Benelux representative."[39]

It was not a very satisfactory response to this forerunner of General de Gaulle's famous "Memorandum on the Directory" (1958).[40] The United States preferred not to be drawn into a three-way consultative club with Britain and France, as Bidault was suggesting. In addition, the United States wanted first to see if the governments of the Western Union would be able to form themselves into an effective grouping. It was only later that the Americans would discover that nothing was possible without them.

Bidault was not the only one who considered that the power represented by the countries he was trying to bring together—to use his words[41]—was insufficient. From all sides—French, British, American—the prevailing impression was that the Brussels Pact represented only an intermediate stage. In a memorandum on January 27, 1948, only five days after Bevin had announced the idea of a new pact to the House of Commons, the British ambassador in Washington, Lord Inverchapel, stated that Bevin visualized that the grouping together of Great Britain, France, and the Benelux countries in a treaty system should be considered a step toward the unity of Europe, "pending the adoption of a wider scheme in which the United States would play their part."[42]

Inverchapel's memorandum transmitted a request by Bevin to Marshall that talks be held between the British and the Americans on the overall question of Western security. These would be, as he had suggested to General Marshall in December 1947,[43] on the model of the previous Anglo-American talks on the Middle East: joint meetings of diplomats and senior military officers of the two countries.[44]

The Treaty of Brussels creating the Western Union of Britain, France, and the Benelux countries was signed on March 17, 1948. In the end, the French point of view generally prevailed. In spite of the preferences of the British, the possibility of future German aggression was retained in the preamble ("to take such steps as may be necessary in the event of a renewal by Germany of a policy of aggression").[45] The desire of the Benelux countries for a move toward economic cooperation was only partially satisfied. The signatories merely accepted the principle of coordination and nonconflict in their economic policies. Neither the British nor, to a lesser extent the French, wanted to set up economic links that could interfere with the progress of the Organization for Economic Cooperation in Europe (OECE). Finally, there was no reference in the treaty text to "spiritual affinities" among the countries of Western Europe.

What was really new in the Treaty of Brussels, and this still counts today, although essentially in a theoretical way, was the principle of "automatic response," which was evoked in the preceding Dunkirk Treaty, although in the latter, as we have seen, it was accompanied by more ambiguous language in another part of the treaty.[46] According to Article 4 of the Treaty of Brussels:

If any of the High Contracting Parties should be the object of an armed attack in Europe, the other High Contracting Parties will, in accordance with the provisions of Article 51 of the Charter of the United Nations, afford the party so attacked all the military and other aid and assistance in their power.[47]

One of the ironies of the Brussels Pact was that, although it was stimulated by the British, and in particular by Ernest Bevin, who claimed to want France returned to its status as a great power[48] (under, of course, the benevolent tutelage or at least the watchful eye of Great Britain), it resulted in the start of a communitarian process in Europe that was opposite of what the British wanted. Following the May 1948 conference at The Hague of European federalist associations, chaired by Winston Churchill, during which the idea of a European Assembly was aired, the logical European institution that could step in and implement it was the newly created Brussels Pact. A year later, the European Assembly idea, and with it the concept of the unity of Europe, took shape, albeit vaguely, with the creation of the Council of Europe. Only reluctantly did the British finally agree to the idea of the council, which was to become a loose association of European states focused on human rights issues. One can say, therefore, that the British initiative that led to the creation of the Brussels Pact eventually was taken over by the French.

Another irony of the Treaty of Brussels was that this pact was supposed to become a system of defense for Europe. Instead, the pact led inexorably to a weakened Europe drawn into a mechanism of military integration under the sponsorship of the United States. As Maurice Vaïsse put it recently,

Europe has tried to construct a defense since the Second World War. She has not succeeded in this. This is the drama that took place when the Cold War broke out and when the countries of Western Europe tried to form a group. But when France and England, plus the Benelux, came together in 1948 to form the Western Union, in fact it amounted to a deficit; that is, these countries did not have the capability, particularly in the military area, to confront the extraordinary Soviet Army. As a result they appealed at that moment to America, and from that time onward, the defense of Europe, which could have been built with solely the contributions of the European countries, systematically [involved] calling upon the United States; and even when it was a question of the creation of the European Defense Community [in the 1950s]—the famous European Army—it was very clear that this European Army was to be part of the Atlantic Pact. And therein lies the problem: why is it that the Europeans cannot manage to defend themselves alone?[49]

On March 17, the day of the signature of the Brussels Pact, President Truman took notice of the event before the Congress: The meaning, he said, "Goes well beyond the provisions of the accord itself. It is an important step in the direction of European unity. . . . This development merits our full support."[50]

Then Truman added, in an understated fashion, "I am confident that the United States, by appropriate means, will provide to the free nations of the world the support required by the situation." In other words, from the very beginning the question arose of an enlargement of the Brussels Pact. The United States could not let the other countries of Europe, particularly the Scandinavian countries, who were outside the "automatic response" provision of the Brussels Pact, to be threatened by the Soviets.

The Brussels Pact, coming on the heels of the Prague coup in February 1948, constituted for France, and for Europe, the decisive step in the road that led from the Victory to NATO. In contrast to the Treaty of Dunkirk and to the various pacts signed between the Soviet Union and its East European satellites, the Treaty of Brussels was the first one not directed exclusively against Germany. On the contrary, it was directed implicitly against the Soviet Union. Therefore, the Communist propaganda machinery reacted against it—with contempt. The Communist weekly, *Tagblatt am Montag* of Vienna, citing the "war of nerves unleashed by the powers of the West," stated:

Moscow is replying to the speech of Truman and the Western [Union] Pact by demobilizing. The increase in the military force of the United States by the application of this Pact is highly problematical. Of all the contracting powers, England is reality the only one that has an army worthy of the name. The others . . . signify absolutely nothing from the military point of view. They possess neither armies nor war industries. They don't have qualified cadres: those who come from the former army completely proved their incompetence during the last war.[51]

Indeed, no one was more keenly aware of the military weakness of the Brussels Pact countries than the signatories themselves. In a joint message to Secretary of State Marshall on April 17, 1948, Bevin and Bidault stated, "We shall require the assistance of the United States, in order to organize the effective defense of Western Europe which at present cannot stand alone."[52]

THE "ANGLO-SAXON TALKS" OF THE SPRING OF 1948

The Anglo-American talks suggested by Bevin[53] opened on March 22, 1948, five days after the conclusion of the Brussels Pact. *Nolens volens*, the British "screen" between the French and the Americans was in operation. At the first session of this military-diplomatic group, to which the Canadians were added, the suggestion of the British delegate Sir Gladwyn Jebb to invite the French was rejected by the Americans. It was necessary first of all, said the Americans, to be assured of French reliability in security matters.[54] It is interesting to point out that Donald McLean, who was later unmasked as a Soviet spy, was present in the British delegation as notetaker throughout this series of top secret "Anglo-Saxon" talks.[55]

The political-military discussions, which extended over six sessions from March 22 to April 1, involved nothing less than the creation of a defensive alliance of the Western countries against the Soviet threat. Just after the conclusion of these meetings, a document of the Joint Chiefs of Staff, dated April 6, 1948,[56] advocated that a démarche be made to the Brussels Pact signatories in favor of a profound transformation of the treaty. The document, according to its preamble, was intended to give substance to President Truman's declaration before the Congress on March 17, 1948, in which he gave assurances that the countries of the Free World would be protected.[57]

The final version of this document of the Joint Chiefs of Staff, which is known as the "Pentagon paper,"[58] is carried as an annex to the report of the final session of the "Anglo-Saxon" talks in Washington. Further, the

Pentagon paper was presented as the result of the work of this group, thus indicating that the direction of the activity was in the hands of the Americans. The paper is proof, if such were needed, that the Americans had come around to the view that the Western Union would not be capable of standing alone. From the beginning of the talks, the Americans, seconded by the British, expressed a desire to extend the European Union to the other countries of Western Europe without delay. The view from Washington was that the five powers of the Brussels Pact were to constitute the hard core of what would become a larger grouping of most of Western Europe.

According to the recommendations of the Pentagon paper, the five signatories of the Treaty of Brussels would be informed officially of a plan to draw up a collective defense agreement for the North Atlantic region. At the same time, these five signatories would be asked to authorize the extension of the treaty to Norway, Sweden, Denmark, Iceland, and Italy. Once this authorization was obtained, an approach would be made to the five candidate countries by the United States, Great Britain, and France. The five governments would be asked if they wanted to be part of the Brussels Pact and at the same time whether they wanted to join in the negotiations for a collective defense agreement for the North Atlantic region.

Following these steps, and again according to the recommendations of the Pentagon paper, President Truman would announce that he was inviting all these countries, plus Canada, Ireland, and Portugal, to take part in negotiations for the creation of the new North Atlantic Pact. Pending the conclusion of this pact, the United States would guarantee the security of the countries of the North Atlantic region against an armed aggression. Finally—and this paragraph of the document had to remain secret—three other countries would be invited at an appropriate moment to participate in the Brussels Pact and the North Atlantic Treaty: Germany and Austria (or at least their three Western occupation zones—British, French, and American), and Spain.

According to a draft paper submitted to the "Anglo-Saxon" talks on March 24, 1948, the reason for the restriction of the area of the new pact to the "North Atlantic" was

to prevent efforts of Latin America, Australia, etc. to adhere, which would make the arrangement unwieldy, especially as none of these are now directly threatened by Soviet Communism. The suggestion would be made that all free nations should eventually be covered by regional security pacts, to the ultimate end that [the UN Charter's] Article 51 security arrangements would be obtained for all free nations.[59]

Although not all of the recommendations of the Pentagon paper, which emerged from the "Anglo-Saxon" talks in Washington were adopted, the

essential element was preserved, namely that a new treaty would be ne-
gotiated for the North Atlantic region.

THE BILLOTTE CHANNEL

According to John Young, on March 16–17, 1948, Ernest Bevin informed Georges Bidault, as well as Prime Minister Robert Schuman and
Interior Minister Jules Moch, that the "Anglo-Saxon" talks were about to
begin in Washington. Schuman, apparently not concerned, replied that in
any case France had its own representatives in Washington—presumably
a reference to the mission of Gen. Pierre Billotte. If Schuman thought that
Billotte's military discussions were the equivalent of the "Anglo-Saxon"
talks he was clearly mistaken.[60]

It seems evident that the French were out of the play. On April 29,
1948, almost a month after the end of the "Anglo-Saxon" talks, Schuman
sent a letter to Secretary of State Marshall proposing that an overall strategy be secretly developed among the United States, Great Britain, and
France. It was only after the elaboration of strategic directives, stated
Schuman, that the discussions in London following the Brussels Pact could
take shape.

In his letter, Schuman thanked Marshall for having arranged for secret
conversations to take place between General Billotte and American military authorities. He expressed the hope that these discussions would be
concluded shortly. He noted in passing that in France, the prime minister
is the person in charge of all matters having to do with national defense.[61]

At this point, it is worth pointing out the marked difference in style and
procedure, in matters of defense as well as others, between the provisional
government headed by General de Gaulle and the governments of the
Fourth Republic that followed. Two examples of Fourth Republic prac-
tices come to mind. On January 29, 1948, an emissary from General Eisenhower (in the latter's role as chief of staff of the Army) came to France
for meetings with French officials. Not only did the emissary, Maj. Gen.
Harold R. Bull, meet with Defense Minister Pierre-Henri Teitgen, but
Bidault, the foreign minister was present as well. Secondly, a French general, Pierre Billotte, held secret discussions with senior American military
authorities, and the French chief of state was not officially informed of
these talks.

The letter that Prime Minister Schuman sent to General Marshall on
April 29, 1948, did not go through diplomatic channels but by a parallel
circuit, which went from Billotte to his interlocutor, General Ridgway, who
forwarded it to the Pentagon. In the Pentagon, it was received by Gen.
Albert Wedemeyer, director of Plans and Operations of the Army Staff,
who sent it to Secretary of State Marshall with a cover letter.[62]

In his cover letter, Wedemeyer informed Marshall that he had temporarily taken over the contact with Billotte during the absence of General Ridgway, who was attending the Bogotá Conference of Inter-American States belonging to the Rio Pact. Billotte was referred to in the cover letter under the code name of "Mr. Ward," and Wedemeyer gave the following account:

Upon his return from Bogotá, General Ridgway visited me and I explained that I had held three meetings with Mr. Ward in each instance at his, Mr. Ward's, request. Mr. Ward wanted to plan specifically for military commitments on the part of France and of the United States. I told General Ridgway that I indicated to Mr. Ward that I was only making exploratory examination of the French capabilities under various premises. I emphasized the need for security and Mr. Ward appeared to understand.[63]

The talks in London to which Schuman referred in his letter of April 29 to Marshall were those taking place as a follow-up to the creation of the Brussels Pact.[64] The next day, April 30, the defense ministers of the Brussels Five (the five signatories) announced in London the creation of a military committee.[65] This committee would serve as the "working party" for the defense ministers' meetings but would also be under the control of the Permanent Commission of the Pact.[66] This commission, based in London, as was to be the military committee, had the function of acting as a continuing entity between meetings of the Consultative Council, which was the supreme body of the Brussels Pact and in effect the Council of Ministers of the Five. The meetings of the Consultative Council were to be held every three months on a rotation basis in the different capitals of the Five.

Apart from these permanent bodies of the Western Union located in London, there also was to be created a headquarters for the military forces of the pact. This would be at Fontainebleau, near Paris, a headquarters that was eventually to become swallowed up by NATO.

NOTES

1. François Mitterrand, *Mémoires Interrompus* (Paris: Odile Jacob, 1996), 38.
2. Ibid., 24.
3. While the French wanted to see a peace treaty concluded among the Big Four powers concerning Germany, they did not like the fact that Byrnes's speech "was a move in the direction of a centralized Germany," in the words of the French chargé in Washington, Armand Bérard (*Foreign Relations of the United States* (FRUS) (1946), vol. 5 *The British Commonwealth: Western and Central Europe* (Washington, D.C.: Government Printing Office, 1969), 694.
4. FRUS (1947), vol. 2, *Council of Foreign Ministers; Germany and Austria* (1972), 813–815.
5. Ibid., 815.

6. Ibid., 816.

7. Ibid.

8. Ibid., 816–17.

9. FRUS (1948), vol. 3, *Western Europe* (1974), 1.

10. Ibid., 2.

11. See p. 30, Chapter 2.

12. Georges-Henri Soutou, "La securité de la France dans l'après-guerre," in *La France et l'OTAN, 1949–1996*, ed. Maurice Vaïsse, Pierre Mélandri, and Fréd-éric Bozo (Brussels: Éditions Complexe, 1996), 34. N.B. As related by Soutou, the text of Bidault's message is contained in an aide-mémoire of General Billotte of December 29 (*Archives Nationales*, Bidault Papers, 457 AP 25).

13. FRUS (1948), 3: 3–6.

14. Great Britain, *Parliamentary Debates, House of Commons*, 446 H.C. DEB, January 20–February 6, 1948 (London: His Majesty's Stationery Office, 1948), 396.

15. Ibid., 392.

16. Ibid., 395–96.

17. *Archives of the Quai d'Orsay* (AQ), Europe 1944–1960, Généralités (Bloc occidental), Dossier 21, Alliance occidentale: Pacte de Bruxelles et Défense de l'Europe February 5–March 13, 1948, note of March 7 by Jean Chauvel, 8. The term "Holy Alliance" refers to the coalition of European monarchies aimed at preventing the spread of French republicanism in the post-Napoleonic period. More generally, it connotes the invocation of religion in carrying out foreign pol-icy—a notion which is unacceptable to the secular tradition that emerged from the French Revolution.

18. FRUS (1948), 3: 7.

19. Ibid.

20. This concept was contained in the famous "long telegram" that Kennan wrote from Moscow in November 1946 and that later appeared in a public version in *Foreign Affairs* of July 1947 entitled "The Sources of Soviet Conduct," and signed by "X."

21. FRUS (1948), 3: 7–8.

22. François Furet, *Le passé d'une illusion: essai sur l'idée communiste au XXe siècle* (Paris: Robert Laffont/Calmann-Lévy, 1995) 440.

23. Ibid., 421.

24. Ibid., 424.

25. Ibid., 198.

26. Lecture by Prof. Bernard Bailyn, Harvard University, 1995.

27. Jacques Godechot and Robert Palmer, "The Problem of the Atlantic," in *Storia Contemporanea, Tenth International Congress of Historical Sciences* (Flor-ence: G. C. Sansoni, 1995), 5: 173–239.

28. Ibid., 175–76.

29. Ronald Steel, *Walter Lippmann and the American Century* (Boston: Little, Brown, 1980), 409.

30. Ibid., 407–8.

31. Godechot and Palmer, "The Problem of the Atlantic," p. 189.

32. Ibid., 191.

33. William R. Keylor, *The Twentieth Century World: An International History* (New York: Oxford University Press, 1996), 191.

34. FRUS (1947), 2: 814.

35. Scott D. Parrish and Mikhail Narinsky, "New Evidence on the Soviet Rejection of the Marshall Plan, 1947: Two Reports," Working Paper No. 9, *Cold War International History Project* (Washington, D.C.: Woodrow Wilson Center, 1995), 34.

36. *National Archives II* (NA II), State Department Files 840.20/3–448, Paris Telegram 1158 to State, March 4, 1948, 3.

37. Ibid., 4.

38. Ibid., 6.

39. Ibid., State Telegram 784 to Paris, March 12, 1948, 1.

40. In September 1958, shortly after his return to power, de Gaulle proposed a strategic directory of the United States, Britain, and France that would come up with decisions on policy, including nuclear policy. The suggestion was not taken up by the Anglo-Americans.

41. See top of p. 42.

42. FRUS (1948), 3: 14.

43. See p. 36, this chapter.

44. FRUS (1948), 3: 15.

45. *American Foreign Policy; Basic Documents, 1950–1955*, vol. 1, Pt. VI, European Regional Arrangements (Washington, D.C.: Government Printing Office, 1957), 968. This language was removed when the Brussels Treaty was modified on October 23, 1954, to allow for the entry of West Germany and Italy into what was re-baptized as the Western European Union (WEU).

46. See p. 22, Chapter 2.

47. *American Foreign Policy, 1950–1955*, 969. N.B. When the Brussels Treaty was modified in October 1954, Article 4 became Article 5. For the pertinent portion of the text of Article 51 of the UN Charter, see Note 59.

48. FRUS (1947), 2: 816. See also p. 36, this chapter.

49. "Le téléphone sonne," *France-Inter*, February 8, 1996.

50. FRUS (1948), 3: 54–55.

51. AQ, Dossier 23, March 15–April 3, 1948, Telegram from French minister in Vienna to Foreign Minister Bidault, March 22.

52. FRUS (1948), 3: 91.

53. See p. 36, this chapter.

54. FRUS (1948), 3: 59–60. This preoccupation with presumed French laxity in security matters appears as a leitmotif in American official documents going back to the relationship between the Roosevelt administration and the Free French movement during the Second World War. It emerges repeatedly in the words of Franklin Roosevelt and of his close advisers such as Robert Murphy.

55. John W. Young, *France, the Cold War and the Western Alliance* (Leicester, U.K.: Leicester University Press, 1990), 182.

56. NA II, Files of the Joint Chiefs of Staff (JCS), CD6–2-43, April 6, 1948.

57. See p. 44, this chapter.

58. FRUS (1948), 3: 72.

59. Ibid., 67. N.B. Article 51 states in part, "Nothing in the present Charter shall impair the inherent right of individual or collective self-defense if an armed attack occurs against a Member of the United Nations, until the Security Council

has taken the measures necessary to maintain international peace and security." Article 52, dealing with regional arrangements, states in part, "Nothing in the present Charter precludes the existence of regional arrangements or agencies for dealing with such matters relating to the maintenance of international peace and security as are appropriate for regional action, provided that such arrangements or agencies and their activities are consistent with the Purposes and Principles of the United Nations."

60. Young, *France, the Cold War and the Western Alliance*, 182.

61. NA II, State Department Files, 740.00/19 Control (Germany) /5–448, April 29, 1948.

62. According to Pierre Gerbet, it was Wedemeyer, along with Ambassador Patrick Hurley, who had done their best to prevent the political re-emergence of France in Indochina at the end of the war. Wedemeyer and Hurley continued to follow Franklin Roosevelt's instructions to this effect even after the president's death (Pierre Gerbet, *Le relèvement, 1944–1949* [Paris: Imprimerie Nationale, 1991], 194). As of mid-1945, Wedemeyer was in charge of Allied forces in Southeast Asia above the 16th parallel.

63. FRUS (1948), 3: 110.

64. There were also diplomatic talks going on in London regarding Germany. These began on April 23, recessed on May 5, and resumed on May 20. They resulted in the London Accords, announced on June 7, whereby the French agreed to merge their zone of occupation in Germany with the British and American zones.

65. FRUS (1948), 3: 146.

66. Ibid., 144.

CHAPTER 4

The Turn toward Washington: The North Atlantic Treaty

THE WASHINGTON EXPLORATORY TALKS

The first task assigned to the new Military Committee of the Brussels Pact was to reply to questions posed on April 19, 1948, by Under Secretary of State Robert Lovett, regarding the availability and disposition of the armed forces on the continent and the defense plans for them, a necessary step before a decision could be made on American military support.[1] This was a further demonstration of the fact, as if this were needed, that the Western Union was never an independent organization.

The Americans were following a procedure that was in the pattern of the economic aid under the Marshall Plan and which had worked so well in the previous year of 1947. Before drawing up military plans, however, the Europeans, especially the French, would have preferred to know in advance the extent of the American military engagement in Europe, especially in terms of assistance in equipment. The French, who found themselves on the front line facing the Russian threat, wanted the United States to commit itself firmly to furnish arms to the countries of Western Europe.

As it turned out, the Military Committee came up with a response to the United States very quickly—on May 12, 1948—and following this demonstration of seriousness of purpose, Senator Arthur Vandenberg introduced on May 19 the resolution that laid the basis for U.S. participation in arrangements for collective defense with other regional organizations. On June 11, the U.S. Senate passed a report commending this resolution, which stated in part:

The experience of World War I and World War II suggests that the best deterrent to aggression is the certainty that immediate and effective counter measures will be taken against those who violate the peace. The principle of individual and collective self-defense is fundamental to the independence and integrity of the United Nations. This is recognized in Art. 51 [of the UN Charter]. By reaffirming now its allegiance to this principle, the USA would take an important step in the direction of removing any dangerous uncertainties that might mislead potential aggressors. Such a reaffirmation is directed against no one and threatens no one. It is solely directed against aggression.[2]

Following the passage of the Vandenberg resolution in June 1948 by the U.S. Senate, talks began with the objective of drawing up the new North Atlantic Treaty. These were called the "Washington Exploratory Talks"—the successor, in effect, of the Anglo-Saxon talks of March/April 1948. The Washington Exploratory Talks were in the course of the negotiations renamed the "Washington Security Talks." The countries represented in this new series of talks were the United States, Great Britain, France, the Netherlands, Belgium, and Canada. Later, Norway joined the talks. In all, there were eighteen sessions of these talks between their inception on July 6, 1948, and the conclusion of the North Atlantic Treaty on April 4, 1949.

We will return to the Washington Exploratory Talks and the drafting of the North Atlantic Treaty presently. But first, we must make a detour through the Brussels Pact command arrangements, which were put in place in the summer and fall of 1948.

THE BRUSSELS PACT COMMAND ARRANGEMENTS

As the meshing of the Brussels Pact with the future North Atlantic alliance became a central preoccupation in the spring and summer of 1948, the French government put forward its objectives in a telegram from Foreign Minister Bidault to Secretary of State Marshall on June 29, 1948. These can be summarized in the following three points:

1. France should participate in meetings of the Combined Chiefs of Staff and on an equal basis with the American and British military officers.
2. A liaison should be set up between Washington and the Military Committee of the Brussels Pact in London. Preferably, an American officer should be assigned to the Military Committee as an observer.
3. Since the field of action is in Germany, a single military commander should be named for all the Allied forces there.[3]

From this list, we can see that the French were prepared to accept a single commander for the forces in Europe; that the commander could be an American (but not British); and that they would expect in return that

France would be granted a place of equal status in the Combined Chiefs of Staff, which they saw as the highest body of Allied military strategy.

Behind Bidault's points can be discerned a fundamental incompatibility between the two ancient rivals of Europe—Britain and France—regarding what strategy to pursue for the defense of their continent. This had to do both with differences of perspective and with national ambitions. In brief, the French government, or at least that government in the person of Bidault, was willing to subordinate itself to the United States, both for its own security and as a means of getting out from under an inferior position vis-à-vis the British.

Anglo-French incompatibility is reflected clearly in another document, a memorandum of the Quai d'Orsay dated April 30, 1948, which described the differences in the following terms:

Great Britain, since the war, has enjoyed an undisputed superiority over the other nations of Europe, with the creation of the Anglo-American Combined Chiefs of Staff.... As a result, British policy consists of:
—on the one hand sparing no effort to become the arms courtier between the United States and the allies of Continental Europe.
—on the other hand, assuming sole command of military operations on the Continent. The initiatives of Marshal Montgomery ... [and] the unofficial notes conveyed to the American press ... tending to demonstrate that the Combined Chiefs of Staff is the only body which can assure coordination between the U.S. and the [Brussels] Five, through the intermediary of the British representation, are among the indications that this policy is being freely put into practice.[4]

According to the memorandum of the Quai d'Orsay, there were two defensive strategies that could be envisaged: One was not to engage troops on the Continent but to transform the British Isles into a vast aircraft carrier, which would constitute a platform for eventual offensive operations; the other was aimed at conducting a delaying operation on the continent pending the arrival of reinforcements. In the second hypothesis, the document stated that "it is clear that the attitude of the American supreme command would be completely modified.... France would take on, in the domain of military action, and in the eyes of the U.S., an importance which has not been accorded to it for the last ten years."[5]

The document of the Quai concluded that French policy should work toward "gaining acceptance by the United States Supreme Command of the second hypothesis." In order to accomplish this, "We should not accept the position of a docile and deferential second.... In the interest of our national policy as well as in the interest of Western Europe, the Combined Chiefs of Staff should be enlarged to include a French representative who would be the equal of his British colleague."[6]

This quest for parity with the British was the principal imperative of the

French during this entire period, and it was the first point raised by Bidault in his memorandum to Marshall on June 29, 1948.[7] This desire of the French was never fully satisfied, in the sense of an effective three-way consultation at the summit, in a civil or military context.

The United States maintained to the French that the Combined Chiefs of Staff was an organization that was more or less defunct. However, the French knew better: A French military publication noted that on September 12, 1946, President Truman had publicly stated that the Anglo-Canadian-American Combined Chiefs of Staff would remain without a change of status until an official declaration that a state of war no longer existed.[8] As for the British, they simply did not want to include the French: It would have undermined their "special relationship" as the most privileged partner of the United States.

By contrast, the second and third points raised by Bidault in his memorandum to Marshall—points that were aimed at loosening the grip that the British held over the structures of the Western Union at London—were looked upon favorably by the United States. In mid-July 1948, the respected Gen. Lyman Lemnitzer was sent by Washington as an observer at the meetings of the Military Committee of the Brussels Pact in London. On August 23, 1948, the United States took a position in favor of a unified command for the Allied forces in Germany. Not wanting to take the lead, the United States decided to reserve a place for the later inclusion of an American officer as deputy commander in chief. These propositions were contained in a memorandum from Marshall to President Truman on August 23. Marshall asked for Truman's approval of these proposals in advance of a meeting which was to take place in London the following day in which the five members of the Brussels Pact were to make decisions regarding the organization of their military forces. Marshall stated that

we support the nomination of a supreme commander for the Western Union from among the following list: Montgomery, Alexander, or the French General Juin, who is currently in Morocco. It is probable that the French are not going to nominate Gen. Juin but instead another officer who is not as good. We consider that, in view of these circumstances, and considering the extreme difficulty that an outbreak of hostilities would present, a man with a strong personality such as Montgomery would probably be preferable.

. . . We are all agreed at this point that, in the period of the outbreak of hostilities, if this should happen, it would not be advisable to have an American commander. Incidentally, the British are insisting that the commander be an American.

We will take a reservation concerning the utilization . . . of the strategic air forces, which will be the most powerful arm and which will be almost entirely American.[9]

Truman immediately replied to Marshall: "I approve your suggestion of today. However, I think we must be very attentive so as not to allow a

foreign commander to use up our troops before he engages himself totally."[10]

Although the text of Marshall's memorandum was somewhat ambiguous
regarding the choice of a supreme commander, one wonders what would
have been the position of the secretary of state if he had not had the
impression that the French government did not want to nominate General
Juin. Whatever the case may be, the die was cast. Once the nomination
of Montgomery was accepted by the United States, it was the beginning
of a new French-British misunderstanding.

The French officer "not as good" as Juin, cited in Marshall's memorandum, was clearly Gen. Jean de Lattre de Tassigny. De Lattre, who was
not particularly close to General de Gaulle, and at the same time had the
confidence of President Auriol, was to be offered the position of commander of the land forces under Marshal Montgomery, following the refusal of Juin to be appointed to this subordinate position. Juin, in declining
the post, noted that his counterparts commanding the air and naval forces
were a grade below him. But obviously the main factor was that he would
not be commander in chief.

The meeting in London to which Marshall referred in his memorandum
to Truman[11] was that of the chiefs of staff of the countries belonging to
the Brussels Pact. Their recommendations were adopted in September by
the defense ministers of the Five.[12] According to the journal of Vincent
Auriol, the defense ministers, who met in Paris on September 27 and 28,[13]
decided at that time to create a "committee" of commanders in chief
headed by a "president":

In the face of the clear desire of the United States not to get further involved at
this point, the five ministers deferred the naming of a Chief of Staff and decided,
as a provisional alternative, to create a committee of commanders in chief (of
land, sea and air forces), with a president who would be a British general officer.[14]

Thus, a muddled arrangement resulted from the United States' continued reluctance to take charge of Europe's security. When it became clear
that the Americans did not want to take the lead, the British apparently
decided that they preferred to have one of their own as commander in
chief. Marshal Montgomery was approaching retirement age and was a
difficult personality, but he was available and enjoyed great prestige from
the war. One would assume that from the British point of view, it would
be better not to have their troops under the orders of a French supreme
commander, especially after the experience of the Battle of France in 1940:
Not having been defeated during the war, they did not want to place
themselves under the command of a military establishment that had been.

From the French point of view, there was the same reflex of rejection.
In truth, it was a curious choice to have a British officer leading an op-

eration of continental defense in which London had declined to make a commitment of a significant number of troops! So instead of a British supreme commander, a less imposing formulation was arrived at—that of a British presidency of a committee of commanders-in-chief.

If the Americans alone had the power of decision, they might have chosen General Juin. However, in the immediate aftermath of the war, the British still enjoyed a sort of psychological parity with the Americans militarily, and it was not until later, with the nuclearization of the alliance and the debacle at Suez, that the British fell into a subordinate position. It is even possible that the Americans may have hinted to Juin beforehand that he might get the supreme commander position. There is a curious reference in Auriol's journal, that expresses his astonishment at the refusal of Juin, "who seems to have gone back on an acceptance which he had virtually given."[15] Though Auriol did not specify the position that had been mooted to Juin, it is doubtful that the latter would ever have accepted a position subordinate to Montgomery, given that the bulk of the troops for the defense of Europe would be French.

One can detect from Auriol's journal a clear bias against Juin. What he seems to have reproached Juin for in particular was the latter's meeting with Marshal Goering in Berlin in December 1941. The object of the meeting was to discuss the consequences of a possible retreat by Gen. Erwin Rommel into Tunisia. Auriol claimed in his journal that Juin took the initiative for this meeting over the head of the Government of Vichy,[16] but there appears to be no proof of this.[17] Juin returned from the meeting in Berlin shocked by the harshness of Goering's manner.[18] (The Berlin meeting seems to have followed on the heels of a meeting in France between Goering and Marshal Pétain, also in December 1941, and there may have been a connection between the two events).

Auriol's mention of the Juin-Goering meeting was in the context of a recommendation of the Quai d'Orsay that Juin be sent on a goodwill mission to the United States. Auriol rejected this idea, not knowing, as he put it, what Juin might concoct in the United States together with General Billotte, whom he described as "in reality the representative of General de Gaulle in the United States." If Juin made the trip to the United States, Auriol opined, he would certainly act to undermine the position of General de Lattre.[19]

American general officers, particularly General Marshall, had high respect for General Juin as the archetypical soldier, although sometimes given to blunt language. Indeed Gen. Bedell Smith, chief of staff to Eisenhower, once remarked to an American military interviewer that if an American officer had talked to him the way Juin had, he would have knocked him down. Eisenhower appeared to corroborate this description of Juin, as he penned beside Smith's statement in the interview, "He sure got his number."[20]

Smith may have been thinking of the incident that arose from the French refusal to obey American orders to withdraw their troops from Strasbourg during the Battle of the Bulge. De Gaulle thought it would be disastrous politically and psychologically for the French to pull out of the capital of Alsace after having liberated it. In this dispute, in which the French won their point, Smith and Juin were acting as seconds to Eisenhower and de Gaulle, and de Lattre, the French commander at Strasbourg, was caught in the middle.

It is a curious footnote of history that Juin, de Gaulle's "second" in the Strasbourg dispute, not only had outranked de Gaulle before the French defeat in 1940 but was first in his class of 1912 at St. Cyr, well ahead of de Gaulle, who was ranked 13th. De Lattre was in the previous class of 1911.

On October 4, the date on which the curious arrangement called the "Committee of Commanders-in-chief of Western Europe" (otherwise known as WUCOS—Western Union Chiefs of Staff) came into being in London, Secretary of State Marshall met in Paris with Prime Minister Schuman. Said Marshall, "When we first received word of the command [arrangements] envisaged [by the Western Union], we thought initially of adding an American deputy to the Supreme Commander. But if Marshal Montgomery is taking the presidency of the committee, I don't see very well what would be the place of such a deputy."[21]

The American secretary of state expressed his regrets that Juin had refused the post of commander of the land forces:

He was by far the best choice. Very few men have worked with the Allies under such extraordinary conditions, all admire him, and he seems to like them. He is both a great fighter and a great chief. No one could be better than he at creating an army and at using the material at hand.

As for the personality of Gen. [Jean] de Lattre [de Tassigny], I hesitate to say anything. To be completely frank, I do not think he can succeed in this task. We have had great difficulties with him, with Marshal Montgomery too, but of a different nature. Gen. de Lattre is very hard to put up with, I know, because I was in contact with him when he made all sorts of complaints to us. I do not see him as a commander of a combined force . . . the contrast with Gen Juin is great.[22]

No one contested the military qualities of de Lattre. Alone among the senior French officers in unoccupied France, he had rebelled against the German takeover in November 1942 and had been imprisoned by the Vichy regime. He later escaped and led the French forces participating in Operation Anvil—the invasion of southern France in August 1944. In the subsequent battle of Alsace, according to Jean Lacouture, the leading biographer of General de Gaulle, de Lattre "handled things with a talent and energy which de Gaulle was the first to recognize."[23] With de Lattre, it appears to have been rather a question particularly of the way he dealt with foreign personalities.

It is clear from letters of postmortem exchanged a few days later between Juin and the then Minister of Defense, Paul Ramadier, that Juin had been confronted with a fait accompli. Initially, a message was sent by the French government to Juin in Morocco offering him the post of commander of the land forces under Montgomery. Juin flew immediately to Paris (this may have been what Auriol interpreted as a virtual acceptance),[24] but once there, he was denied permission to go to London, the seat of the Western Union, to learn more about the position offered. "You were already too far committed with the British," said Juin in a letter of October 13 to Ramadier, "to have allowed me possibly to obtain by this means conditions more in line with our national preoccupations and with the sacrifices that are expected of us."[25]

In his reference to the "sacrifices which are expected of us," Juin was alluding to the fact that the bulk of the troops would be French. Juin likened the position offered to him to the "subaltern" and "ill-defined" North East Theater command conferred on Gen. Joseph Georges in 1939, but without even the military means that Georges had at his disposal at the time.[26]

As if to chide the government's leaders, and the man chosen in his stead, for their overreliance on their British ally of 1940 (rather than the Americans), Juin drove his point home: "There is nothing to be sorry about. The important point is that General de Lattre be briefed on and be fully conscious himself regarding the desire all Frenchmen not to have to take the road of Dunkirk again."[27]

In his letter, Juin also deplored the lack of cohesion in the French military structure, notably the absence at the time of a chief of staff of national defense; in other words, a military officer who could speak to the government in the name of the armed forces. Juin had previously held this function, under the provisional government of Charles de Gaulle and subsequently until his departure as resident general in Morocco in May 1947. The result of this vaccuum, stated Juin, was a scattering of the military authority into clans.

Ramadier, in a slightly veiled response on October 15, 1948, to Juin's letter of refusal, stated, "I can well understand your refusal of my offer, when the British Government had expressed its desire to maintain the precise and challenging responsibilities which I had conveyed to you, without the attenuation which you envisaged."[28]

It seems clear from this exchange of letters that the British government had already taken a firm position that Marshal Montgomery had to be at the summit of the Western Union command arrangements and that the French government had chosen not to contest this.

WASHINGTON'S DOUBTS ABOUT FRANCE

In his letter to Ramadier, Juin mentioned the unfavorable image of France abroad: "Our internal situation is such as to create considerable suspicion toward us."[29] Presumably he was referring to the torn political atmosphere in France, marked by governmental instability and, in late 1948, by widespread social unrest under the impulsion of the Communist Party, similar to what had taken place at the end of 1947.

As far as Washington was concerned, Juin was basically correct. While it might be too strong to describe it as suspicion, certainly an attitude of reserve toward France was evident. Although at the time (October 1948), the United States had begun to transfer the material necessary to re-equip three French divisions in Germany,[30] some officials expressed doubts about France's reliability. Chief among these was Kenneth C. Royall, secretary of the Army, who was concerned with, among other things, the "disturbing proportion" of the French electorate that was voting Communist.[31] Though overruled by Secretary of Defense James Forrestal, who argued that risks had to be accepted in U.S. alliance relationships,[32] Royall made several remonstrances during the period. In a memorandum to Forrestal on March 14, 1949, Royall quoted from an Army intelligence review of the previous month:

The effectiveness of the French forces is seriously limited at present by several factors: . . . (1) Morale, which has declined, primarily because of low pay, high cost of living, inadequacy of equipment, the debilitating campaign in Indo-China, and an unstable political situation in Metropolitan France; (2) lack of heavy equipment; and (3) weakness in overall administration. Officers, however, are reasonably well trained.

Under present circumstances, the French Army is capable only of maintaining security throughout the French Union, barring widespread disorders. It could not successfully resist a major aggressor.[33]

Royall concluded his memorandum to Forrestal by stating that "I again suggest that the above-mentioned factors be constantly kept in view, particularly with regard to the amount and timing and supervision of foreign military aid to the French."[34]

THE DEBATE OVER THE FUTURE OF THE WESTERN UNION

Behind the inclination of Marshall to favor Juin over de Lattre was the clear preference of the Americans, and in this they were not exceptional, for dealing with someone who did not cause difficulties for them. In Marshall's thinking may have been, however, a wider political appreciation.

De Lattre as the wartime general who complained about not getting equipment was also the leading figure in the postwar French military establishment who, with encouragement from the chief of state, Vincent Auriol, advocated the military separation of Europe from the United States. Their priority was to get a Western European bloc organized militarily, so that it could then absorb the military assistance that the United States would contribute to it.[35] It followed from this that the bloc should retain a political independence, drawing support from its U.S. ally but not getting into a position of dependence. De Lattre wrote the following in a note dated June 20, 1948 on "The Defense of Western Europe":

There is not even a solution in terms of vassalization with respect to America. (The Marshall Plan had the grave inconvenience of placing us in too great a [state of] dependence on America). Vassalization by America will clearly have as its fatal ending a combat between *two* equivalent forces.

In effect, if the Western bloc is organized solely as an American dependency, that will amount to taking a position *a priori*—of simply being at one with America.

The game would be more supple with a Western Europe which sought at least an appearance of independance. But in that case, *the whole German policy* would have to be started from scratch.

It was probably necessary with the Germans, as I thought in 1945, *to show them force* and to hold out a hand to them.[36]

This flexibility that de Lattre (and Auriol) sought for a Western European bloc could extend to taking positions completely independent of both the United States and the Soviet Union. In a speech at the end of July, 1948, de Lattre expressed the hope that "if . . . in spite of our weakness, the French spirit can put together a European strategy and find the means of operating between the two blocs and manage to separate them to avoid igniting the spark, then we will have done our work well."[37]

According to Georges-Henri Soutou, the approach of de Lattre, as reflected in his speech of July 1948 was very close to that of two other key statesmen of the period, Robert Schuman and Jean Monnet, and was widely shared by the diplomats at the Quai d'Orsay—notably Secretary-General Jean Chauvel and the French ambassador to London, René Massigli. They were lined up against the partisans of a close alliance with Washington, which, in the view of the proponents of a Western European bloc, carried the serious risk of aggravating the cold war.[38]

The partisans of a close alliance with Washington included General Juin, General Billotte, General Georges Revers, the chief of staff of the Army, and a number of other senior military officers. They were wary of a tight association between Great Britain and France as represented in the Western Union because it followed from such an association, and the imperative of harmony implied in it, that Britain would play the role of a "screen" between France and the United States. In this curious dialectic, Juin and his ex-deputy Billotte, although both of Gaullist persuasion, were inclined toward direct contacts with Washington. Their reasoning was that American military aid could be obtained more efficiently in direct contacts, and the result would be that France would recover its fighting strength more quickly. "Isn't it counter-indicated," said Juin in his October 13, 1948, letter to Ramadier, "to place a British screen between this European command and Washington, where the key to the situation is located?"[39] Political considerations, such as the need to avoid provoking the Soviets by an overly close relationship with Washington, seem to have been largely absent from the thinking of Juin and the military officers allied with him who included those on the General Staff of National Defense.[40]

As indicated in chapter 2,[41] Juin had from the beginning been an advocate of U.S. military involvement in Europe. As chief of the General Staff of National Defense under the provisional government of de Gaulle, he had endorsed a study by a subordinate, Col. Pierre Lassalle, advocating a direct participation of the United States in the defense of the West. Dated October 22, 1945, this study recommended that there be a single commander for the forces of the West, which would include 450,000 American troops.[42]

What helps explain this paradox of Gaullist-inclined officers, principally Juin and Billotte, seeking a recourse in Washington, was that the alternative, as practiced by the Fourth Republic governments of the time, inevitably placed France into a position inferior to Great Britain in any purely "European" command arrangements. General de Gaulle, then in the opposition as head of the Rally of the French People (RFP), did not hesitate to point this out in his characteristically trenchant manner. In a press conference on March 29, 1949, he attacked the French government's decision to allow the British to take the lead in the organization of the Western Union:

They thought it was a good idea, perhaps to rid themselves of some of the burden, to give the lead to the British if the need arose. I personally think it is the wrong idea to believe that the defense of Western Europe, that is of France, can be centered on England. This is an historic, geographic and strategic error of enormous proportions. England is England, with its values and with its means. It is not the center of Europe.[43]

One can find this difference of appreciation in Auriol's journal, even though clarity of language was not always his strong point. The following is an extract from the journal for October 15, 1948:

What we must obtain from the Americans is an American operation in Europe, with European aid, completely the contrary of what Juin thinks. [Heretofore] England has never agreed to an accord embodying this idea, which consists of fighting in the east; this is an historical fact. [Paul-Henri] Spaak is completely of our opinion; it is necessary to maintain the western pact.[44]

In other words, the fact that Britain had undertook, for the first time in history, to defend the European Continent as far to the east as possible was of overriding importance. Since this commitment had been embodied in the Brussels Pact, it was vital to maintain the separate integrity of the pact. The problem with this approach was that a British treaty guarantee to defend its Continental allies did not mean much, because it was not accompanied by a specific commitment of land forces. (This the British would not promise until after the failure of the European Defense Community in 1954.)

For the "European current," represented by Auriol and Ramadier, it was disturbing that France, by entering the North Atlantic Pact, was to link its foreign policy to that of the United States for years to come. On November 23, 1948, Ramadier, as defense minister, made known his concerns in this regard in a letter to Prime Minister Schuman. Ramadier stressed the theme that the Brussels Pact must maintain its identity despite the creation of the new North Atlantic Pact, as the latter risked constituting a further divisive factor in French politics. It would meet with a resistance in France that the Brussels Pact did not. The Communists had mounted a campaign against the Atlantic Pact that had had an influence well beyond the usual Communist constituencies. Others in the French public would criticize the government for not having safeguarded French sovereignty and having instead put the country's policies under Foreign control.

Ramadier's letter went on to state that the draft text of the Atlantic Pact seemed to grant a right of intervention not unlike that of the Holy Alliance of the past. One could logically counter with the idea of a European Monroe Doctrine in opposition to it. It would be easy to portray the government as having placed France in a protectorate status.

Ramadier further argued that entering into the mutual defense pact would tie the signatories to a common policy, and he questioned whether Europe should tie itself so closely to the U.S. in this manner. The U.S., for example, gets involved in commitments with which the European countries, with their limited resources, cannot become associated. The Brussels Pact implies a deeper association than the Atlantic Pact and therefore should not become subsumed in the Atlantic Pact. Ramadier concluded:

At the least the Five should affirm in some way that the Brussels Pact will be maintained, in its overall political and economic thrust, and in its provision for absolutely automatic response in terms of the [military] assistance to be provided.[45]

THE WASHINGTON TREATY: TAKEOVER BY THE UNITED STATES

Juin's refusal left the position of commander of Western Union ground forces open to General de Lattre, whose bursts of enthusiasm and short span of concentration augured a future incompatibility with the taciturn Marshal Montgomery. In fact, their personal relations became untenable, and de Lattre's complaints about Montgomery to Auriol, reflected in the latter's journal, are a testimony to this.

Montgomery was the president of the Committee of Commanders-in-Chief of Western Europe, otherwise known as Western Union Chiefs of Staff (WUCOS), but this compromise formulation begged the question of whether he really "commanded" the Allied forces in Germany. Particularly galling was not so much Montgomery's presence at the Fontainebleau Headquarters of WUCOS but the fact that a large sum of French government money had been spent to refurbish a chateau for his residence. One can thus characterize the ambiguous period that followed, until the designation at the end of 1950 of a Supreme Allied Commander, Europe (SACEUR), as "waiting for Eisenhower."

It was also a period in which U.S. policy ineluctably underwent a change. At the beginning, after the signing of the Brussels Pact, the United States wanted to help create a grand alliance in Western Europe, which would serve to raise morale on the Continent, already badly shaken by the coup of Prague. The sending of large numbers of American troops to the Continent on a permanent basis was not envisaged. Nor was an American supreme commander over Allied forces in Germany considered advisable. It was only after months of discussions with the parties involved in the new alliance that it was perceived that the Europeans could not get themselves organized, as they had with the Marshall Plan. The Americans then stepped in to take charge, at first reluctantly.

On July 6, 1948, the so-called Washington Exploratory Talks began— the successor, so to speak, of the Anglo-Saxon talks of the spring of 1948. The French delegate at these talks was the ambassador in Washington, Henri Bonnet, whose informative telegrams were read with continuing interest in Paris.

The Washington Exploratory Talks, which later became known as the Washington Security Talks, were concerned with nothing less than the elaboration of a new mutual defense treaty for the North Atlantic region. The decisive step in this process was taken with the decision in principle by the Brussels Pact powers, meeting on October 25–26, 1948, in Paris, to negotiate a treaty for the North Atlantic region with the United States and Canada.[46]

For the French, these exploratory talks, which were to concern in particular the attachment of the Scandinavian countries to the new pact,

aroused anxieties about an equilibrium of influence between the northern
and southern countries of Europe (a not-unfamiliar theme even in the
1990s, with the arrival of northern European countries as new members
of the European Union). France, seeing itself in the frontline of the defense of Western Europe, was insistent on obtaining a U.S. security guarantee and an American commitment to provide military aid. The concern
of the United States not to leave unprotected the peripheral countries such
as Norway (which was subject to veiled Soviet threats) was to the French
a secondary matter.

In the 1948–1949 debate over the shape of the new defensive alliance,
a dialectic is discernable between "enlargement" and "deepening," not
unlike what is found today in the debate about adding new countries to
the European Union. For those in favor of "deepening," there was the
risk of a dispersion of effort. The emphasis, according to this school of
thought, should be on the Western Union as the hard core of the Western
alliance structure. For those who favored enlargement, it was particularly
important to extend the alliance's system of protection, so as to prevent
the Soviets from absorbing the outlying countries one by one.

For the Americans, there was a concern both for coherence and cohesion. The North Atlantic area was large enough to permit the creation of
a regional organization in conformity with the United Nations Charter.[47]
It was not desirable to create a great ensemble of countries going beyond
the North Atlantic region, as this would be like the amorphous Kellog-
Briand Pact of 1928, which revealed itself to be merely declaratory and
totally ineffective.[48] The case of Italy was somewhat special. It was necessary to protect Italy, but was it logical that this country, which was not
part of the North Atlantic region, be included in the new pact? Although
at a certain point, associate member status was considered for Italy and
the so-called stepping-stone countries (Norway, Denmark, Sweden), in the
end it was decided to admit them all as full members—that is, all who
desired to join. Sweden (and also Ireland) did not. For the faraway countries—Greece, Turkey, and Iran—there was a separate Anglo-American
guarantee of security outside the new pact.[49] Finally, to give the Americans
a sense of "added value" in the matter of security, it was decided to include Greenland, which gave France the opportunity to insist that its three
départements on the other side of the Mediterranean, in Algeria, also be
included.

In the elaboration of the final text of the North Atlantic Treaty, especially regarding the key article (Article Five) that deals with the response
to be made in case of an armed attack, American officials had to navigate
between difficult shoals. On the one hand were the French, representing
considerable power within the Atlantic alliance, however virtual. Still far

from recovered from the trauma of the wartime Occupation, the French wanted the strongest possible security guarantee. On the other hand, American planners had to take into account the traditional reflexes of the U.S. Senate, imbued with George Washington's injunction against "entangling alliances" and with the weight of its own 1920 rejection of membership in the League of Nations.

For Article Five, there was a range of choices that went from the "automatic response" formula found in the Brussels Pact—impossible to get past the U.S. Senate—to the formula found in the Rio de Janeiro Treaty of 1947 for the states of the Western Hemisphere: In the event of an armed attack, the "Organ of Consultation" of the pact would meet immediately to agree on the measures to be taken for the common defense and for the peace and security of the hemisphere.

On February 16, 1949, American diplomats arrived at a minimal formula that they wanted to test with the British, in order to get an idea of what the reaction of the various other countries would be, prior to presenting it to the leadership of the Senate. This minimal formula eliminated all reference to the use of armed force. In a memorandum to the Secretary of State, Charles Bohlen, who was at the time counsellor of the department, observed, "We anticipate that this will cause some difficulties, particularly with the French, but believe that in the last analysis it will be sufficiently acceptable to the other countries involved so as not to impair the chief purposes of the pact."[50]

In the final text, the mention of possible military action was included, but it was clearly less binding than in the counterpart article in the Brussels Pact. According to Article Five of the North Atlantic Treaty:

The parties agree that an armed attack against one or more of them in Europe or North America shall be considered an attack against them all, and consequently agree that, if such an armed attack occurs, each of them, in exercise of the right of individual or collective self-defense recognized by Art. 51 of the U.N. Charter, will assist the party or parties so attacked by taking forthwith, individually and in concert with the other parties, such action as it deems necessary, including the use of armed force, to restore and maintain the security of the North Atlantic area.[51]

In March 1949, the final draft of the North Atlantic Treaty was agreed on by the United States, Britain, France, Canada, Belgium, the Netherlands, Luxembourg, and Norway (the latter having taken part in the later stages of the negotiations). The treaty was signed on April 4, 1949, by these eight nations and also by Denmark, Iceland, Italy, and Portugal, which had received invitations to join the pact.[52] Robert Schuman, as foreign minister, signed for France.

GENESIS OF NATO'S STEERING COMMITTEE
(STANDING GROUP)

After the signing of the Washington Treaty, work began on setting up the structures that were to follow after the signing of the pact. The pact created only a council. According to Article Nine of the treaty:

The parties hereby establish a Council, on which each of them shall be represented, to consider matters concerning the implementation of this treaty. The Council shall be so organized so as to be able to meet promptly at any time. It shall set up subsidiary bodies as may be necessary; in particular, it shall establish immediately a Defense Committee.[53]

The French ambassador in Washington, Henri Bonnet, who had warned his fellow participants in the Washington Exploratory Talks of the dangers of a watering-down of Article Five,[54] was also concerned with the structures that were to emerge from the signing of the treaty. On February 14, several weeks before the signing of the North Atlantic Treaty, Bonnet requested of Dean Acheson that France become a full-fledged member of the Anglo-American Combined Chiefs of Staff, the command arrangement that was put in place in World War II. Bonnet added that he knew that this body continued to exist.[55]

Acheson, who had followed General Marshall as secretary of state, reminded Bonnet that General Marshall had already told him that the Combined Chiefs of Staff had not met for two years, that it existed only on paper, and that its present existence was only due to certain matters related to the Second World War.

Strictly speaking, the American affirmations were accurate: the Combined Chiefs of Staff had virtually ceased to exist. The wartime Anglo-American cooperation in the nuclear field had been halted by the MacMahon Act of 1946, which stated that "until Congress declares by joint resolution that effective and enforceable international safeguards against the use of atomic energy for destructive purposes have been established, there shall be no exchange of information with other nations with respect to the use of atomic energy for industrial purposes."[56] (However, the MacMahon Act was later to be modified in the 1950s in favor of Great Britain.[57])

But the reality of the British-American relationship in the postwar period was far different. There was an important British military mission in Washington, and British officers generally had an easy access to the Pentagon. The Department of State recognized this anomaly and stated so in a position that was conveyed from the secretary of defense to the secretary of the army on March 8, 1948:

The French Government has long been hypersensitive about the presence of the British Staff Mission in Washington [and] has a great desire to have similar contact with our military authorities. The difficulties which would be presented by the presence of such a French mission are realized but, if the NME could see its way clear to authorizing the French to send such a mission, this would appear to be the most effective means of influencing French military thought.[58]

Moreover, there was another factor of great importance in the Anglo-American relationship: On September 12, 1945, President Truman had signed a memorandum authorizing, in peacetime, the continuation of Anglo-American exchanges of signals intelligence.[59] In so doing, Truman was responding positively to a memorandum jointly submitted by the secretaries of state, war, and navy, and which stated in part:

Not only were many military and naval victories of the Allies made possible by learning the plans and intentions of the enemy, but also much important diplomatic and economic information, otherwise unobtainable, was furnished to cognizant authorities. . . .

In view of the disturbed conditions of the world and the necessity of keeping informed of technical developments and possible hostile intentions of foreign nations . . . it is recommended that you authorize continuation of collaboration between the United States and the United Kingdom in the field of communications intelligence.[60]

In his conversation with Acheson on February 14, 1949, the French ambassador insisted that France was of an importance such that it should be a member of a tripartite group able to make decisions at the highest level. In this regard, Bonnet suggested that a visit by General Juin, ostensibly to present a decoration to West Point, might be useful.[61]

A response from the Joint Chiefs of Staff was not long in coming, in the person of Gen. Alfred Gruenther (who was later to become Supreme Commander of NATO forces). Dated February 17, 1949, this document demonstrates starkly the gap that separated at that time, and still somewhat separates today, Anglo-American strategists on the one hand and their French counterparts on the other.[62] The following are extracts:

The Joint Chiefs are strongly opposed to anything resembling a tripartite Chiefs of Staff; to having the multinational defense committee of the North Atlantic Pact (in contrast to the more restricted mechanism of the Brussels Pact) . . . take responsibility for formulating coordinated plans for the defense of Western Europe; and to having a French General, whoever it may be, come here in the near future to discuss such matters.

The document continues:

The Joint Chiefs accept the integration of American plans for the defense of Western Europe with the plans of the Western Union, so that in the event of war, the American forces in Western Europe would be under the command of the Western Union. But they reserve to themselves the decision on the size of these [American] forces in relation to other theaters of operations; and they will keep under their control the operation of the strategic arm of the U.S. Air Force.

Putting aside the strategy concerning Western Europe and the communications in the North Atlantic, the Joint Chiefs consider that we have world-wide responsibilities which we have to face as we see fit, and that the British have similar responsibilities, and that as a result, a close coordination with them is desirable; whereas fundamentally the French have responsibilities only in Europe and North Africa. Their capability is not adequate enough to play a role in other theaters of operations and thus they are not qualified to participate in considerations of global strategy.

Thus, the French were excluded from the inner circle of Anglo-American cooperation. But at the same time, any plan for the defense of Europe hinged on France. This dilemma was pointed out in a memorandum from Charles Bohlen, counsellor of the State Department, following a meeting at the Pentagon on March 31, 1949:

It was agreed by all, and particularly forcibly presented by Gen. [Lauris] Norstad, that the nub of the matter was, in effect, the role of France; that no matter what form of organization was set up under the [North Atlantic] Pact, the central problem would remain as to whether or not France could be informed and have an equal voice in the determination of major strategy. Gen. Norstad, in particular, felt that there was a constant danger that the political purposes of this Pact would be destroyed if France felt that she was excluded from the top military planning group; against this, there were strong feelings of the joint British and American staffs that for security reasons alone France could not be cut in on overall strategic planning.[63]

According to a compromise formula suggested by Bohlen, which was accepted in principle, France would take part in the real directing body of the North Atlantic Pact, but all the organizations of the pact would have no other objective than the application of the pact itself. In other words, no organization of the pact would deal with problems of global strategy, such as in the Middle East or the Far East. There would be, then, a Council of the Pact, a Defense Committee, and a Military Committee, on all of which all countries would be represented. Beyond this, there would be a restricted "Steering Committee" (later to become known as the "Standing Group") of the Military Committee, on which there would be France and Great Britain representing the Western Union, plus the United States and Canada.[64]

During this same period, Acheson received a letter from General Wedemeyer, dated March 28, 1949, in which the latter made an evaluation of his contacts with General Billotte and suggested to the secretary of state that these contacts be dropped. The origin of these contacts, stated Wedemeyer, was

an arrangement that was made during General Eisenhower's incumbency as Chief of Staff. General Marshall asked that one officer be designated in the Department of Army to maintain contact with a General Billotte, the French Military Representative in the United Nations at Lake Success. I was designated to fill this liaison role approximately twelve months ago. I have had a few meetings here in Washington with the French General. The French for the past several months had been striving to arrange for staff conferences with American military men. Frequently they suggested that they should be included in the membership of the Combined Chiefs of Staff. However ... it was indicated to the French that the Combined Chiefs of Staff is no longer extant. I was admonished not to make any commitments in my conversations with the French concerning military collaboration. Further, I was told to carry on conversations that would cause the French to feel that at least they had an opportunity to express their military views to someone in Washington. Every two or three months, General Billotte visited my office. We had pleasant conversations, none of which amounted to anything from the American viewpoint; however, he did outline French views concerning the developing strategic situation in Western Europe.[65]

Acheson replied to Wedemeyer that the contact with General Billotte should not be cut off but should continue awhile longer until such point as the status of French officers would be regularized by the creation of the military structures of the North Atlantic Pact.[66]

As we shall see in the next chapter, the creation of the North Atlantic Pact structures provided for a special status for the United States, Britain, and France as members of the Standing Group of the Military Committee. But this arrangement was to fall far short of meeting France's strategic aims.

NOTES

1. *Foreign Relations of the United States* (FRUS) (1948), vol. 3, *Western Europe* (Washington, D.C.: Government Printing Office, 1974), 123–24.

2. Henry W. Degenhardt, ed. *Treaties and Alliances of the World* (Detroit, MI: Gale Research, 1986), 202.

3. FRUS (1948), 3: 142–43.

4. *Archives of the Quai d'Orsay* (AQ), Europe 1944–1960, Généralités (Bloc occidental), Dossier 22, Alliance Occidentale: The Brussels Pact and the defense of Europe, March 15–April 3, 1948. Note on American strategy and Western Europe, April 30, 1948, pp. 5–6.

5. Ibid., 6–7.

6. Ibid., 7.

7. See p. 54, this chapter.

8. *Informations Militaires*, 73 (September 20, 1946): 8.

9. *National Archives II* (NA II), Joint Chiefs of Staff (JCS) Files, CD6–2-49, August 23, 1948. See also FRUS (1948), 3: 221–22.

10. Ibid.

11. See p. 56, this chapter.

12. FRUS (1948), 3: 289–90.

13. Vincent Auriol, *Journal du septennat* (Paris: Armand Colin, 1974), 2: 683 (note 22).

14. Ibid., 460.

15. Ibid.

16. Ibid., 3: 71–72.

17. Ibid., 544 (note 185).

18. Ibid.

19. Ibid., 71–72 (entry of January 28, 1949).

20. Forrest C. Pogue, "The Genesis of the Supreme Command: Personal Impressions of Eisenhower the General," in *Eisenhower: A Centenary Assessment*, ed. Gunter Bischof and Stephen E. Ambrose (Baton Rouge and London: Louisiana State University Press, 1995), 31.

21. AQ, Europe 1944–1960, Généralités (Bloc occidental), Dossier 22, Alliance Occidentale: The Brussels Pact and the Defense of Europe, May 1948–June 1949, Interview between Marshall and Schuman, October 4, 1948, 2.

22. Ibid., 3–4.

23. Jean Lacouture, *De Gaulle vol. 2, Le politique* (Paris: Seuil, 1985), 75.

24. See p. 58, this chapter.

25. Marshal Alphonse Juin, *Mémoires* (Paris: Arthème Fayard, 1960), 2: 169.

26. Ibid., 168. Georges, commander of the Northeast Theater, was in effect the commander of the Battle of France in 1940. At the same time, he was subordinate to the commander-in-chief of the French-British forces, Gen. Maurice Gamelin, who exercised his command from Paris at the Château de Vincennes. In a book published after the war, Gamelin referred to the campaign as "the battle of Gen. Georges."

27. Ibid., 169.

28. Ibid., 170.

29. Ibid., 167.

30. NA II, Joint Chiefs of Staff (JCS) files, CD6–2-4, October 10, 1948.

31. Ibid., March 31, 1949.

32. Ibid., March 18, 1949.

33. Ibid., March 14, 1949.

34. Ibid.

35. Georges-Henri Soutou, "La securité de la France dans l'après-guerre," in *La France et l'OTAN, 1949–1996*, ed. Maurice Vaïsse, Pierre Mélandri and Frédéric Bozo (Brussels: Éditions Complexe, 1996), 35.

36. Jean de Lattre, *Ne pas subir* (Paris: Plon, 1984), 389 (quoted in part in Soutou, "La sécurité de la France," p. 38). Clearly de Lattre was advocating a less intransigent and more flexible French policy toward Germany, one that would draw it into a Western European bloc.

37. Soutou, "La sécurité de la France dans l'après-guerre," 40–41.

38. Ibid., 39.

39. Juin, *Mémoires*, 2: 168.

40. Soutou, "La sécurité de la France dans l'après-guerre," 42.

41. See pp. 17, Chapter 2.

42. Soutou, "La sécurité de la France dans l'après-guerre," 25. Also see p. 17, Chapter 2.

43. Charles de Gaulle, *Discours et Messages, vol. II, 1946–1958, Dans l'attente, Février 1946–Avril 1958* (DM) (Paris: Omnibus/Plon, 1970), 462. (N.B. In this chapter, when the Omnibus/Plon edition is used, the abbreviation OP will so indicate. Otherwise the initial Plon edition is meant).

44. Auriol, *Journal du septennat*, 2: 484. N.B. "Western pact" means the Western Union formed by the Brussels Pact. Paul-Henri Spaak was Belgian prime minister at the time and a leading "Europeanist."

45. Ibid., 601–2.

46. FRUS (1948), 3: 270.

47. For the UN Charter's language on the creation of regional organizations see Note 59, chapter 3.

48. This pact, named after the American secretary of state, Frank Kellog, and the French minister of foreign affairs, Aristide Briand, involved renunciation of aggressive war but made no provision for sanctions. The League of Nations implemented the pact with a general act that included an optional clause involving compulsory arbitration. The latter was accepted by twenty-three nations, in some cases with reservations (William L. Langer, ed., *An Encyclopedia of World History* [Boston: Houghton Mifflin, 1972], 960).

49. Greece and Turkey were admitted into the North Atlantic Pact in February 1952.

50. FRUS (1949), vol. 4, *Western Europe* (1975), 114.

51. Degenhardt, *Treaties and Alliances of the World*, 204.

52. Ibid., 203. (After ratification by all parliaments concerned, the North Atlantic Treaty came into being on August 24, 1949.)

53. Ibid.

54. FRUS (1949), 4: 76.

55. Ibid., 107–8.

56. Public Law 585, 79th Cong., 2d sess. (1 August 1946) Chapter 724, *Atomic Energy Act of 1946* (McMahon Act), 766.

57. There were two modifications of the McMahon Act in the 1950s: on August 30, 1954 (Atomic Energy Act of 1954), Public Law 703, and on July 2, 1958 (Atomic Energy Act of 1958). The latter (Public Law 85–479) authorized *inter alia* passage to a foreign nation of atomic weapons data *"provided that nation has made substantial progress in the development of nuclear weapons"* (emphasis added), which effectively meant only the British, who were much farther along in atomic weapons development than the French.

58. NA II, JCS Files, CD6–2-4, March 8, 1948. (N.B. NME is an acronym for National Military Executive, which is now known as the National Command Authority—NCA).

59. Christopher Andrew, *For the President's Eyes Only* (New York: Harper-Collins, 1990), 162.

60. Ibid., 161–62. (Sourced to Harry S. Truman Presidential Library, Naval Aide Files, box 10, file 1, "Memorandum to the President, Subject: Collaboration with

the British in the Communications Intelligence Field, Continuation and Extension of," September 12, 1945.)

61. FRUS (1949), 4: 107–8.

62. Ibid., 120–21.

63. Ibid., 256. General Norstad was later to become commander of NATO forces in Europe.

64. Ibid., 256–57.

65. FRUS (1949), 4: 294.

66. Ibid., 295.

CHAPTER 5

The Alliance Becomes an Organization: NATO

PREPARATION OF THE ATLANTIC PACT STRUCTURES

With the United States now into the Western alliance system, France considered itself, at least for a time, as no longer a frustrated junior partner of Britain; it was a willing junior partner of the United States. Moreover, the entry of the United States into the scene promised a more vigorous and more serious defense of the Continent than the British were prepared to provide. Also, since the defense of the Continent would require a preponderance of French troops, the role of France would inevitably grow in importance.

From the moment of the signing of the North Atlantic Treaty, the question of the structures of the treaty arose. The relation of these structures to the Brussels Pact became immediate concerns for Allied military planners.

Within the General Staff of National Defense (EMGDN) in Paris, and also at the political level in the French government, the structures of the new Atlantic Pact could be seen as breaking the British monopoly represented in the Combined Chiefs of Staff (CCS) and as correcting an unsatisfactory situation in the command of the Western Union Chiefs of Staff (WUCOS) at Fontainebleau. The latter situation was exemplified by the personality conflict between Montgomery and de Lattre. On August 2, 1949, a note of the permanent staff of the prime minister at the time, Henri Queuille, stated that

the divergence of views between the British High Command and the French High Command are no secret to anyone; to the point where public opinion on both sides of the Atlantic is aware of it and is demanding a solution in the form of the implementation of the Atlantic Pact which if it is not done will severely undermine the cohesion of the West.[1]

Since under the new twelve-member Atlantic Pact, a high-level strategic planning group of that number would be too unwieldy, the idea arose of a "restricted strategic staff" or steering committee, with only a few countries represented. Initially, as we have seen in the previous chapter, these were to be the United States, Great Britain, France, and Canada. In effect, Britain and France would represent the Western Union, and the United States and Canada the Western Hemisphere.

According to a French Defense Ministry note of June 10, 1949, a small directing group would be the answer to the Americans' two major preoccupations: secrecy and efficiency. The question of how the smaller countries would be kept in the picture would have to be worked out. One suggestion was that the French could represent some of the other countries, namely Italy and the Benelux countries, in the deliberations within the restricted group.[2] This was especially true for the Benelux countries, as noted in another Foreign Ministry document two months later: "[Since] the interests of the small states of Western Europe coincide in large measure with those of France, the latter is quite naturally qualified to be their spokesman."[3]

The "restricted" group, in French eyes, was to take the place of the CCS. A French Defense Ministry note of June 10, 1949 stated that "it is necessary for French interests that the new organism be substituted for the Combined Chiefs of Staff. Besides, the continuation of an Anglo-American tête-à-tête would be contrary to the spirit of the Atlantic Alliance."[4]

Moreover, at the time of the signing of the North Atlantic Treaty, Foreign Minister Robert Schuman had received a promise from his counterpart, Secretary of State Dean Acheson, that France would be a member of this restricted strategic group. As the August 2, 1949, note of the prime minister's staff observed, "M. Acheson promised M. Schuman that France would be admitted on an equal basis to the four-power Supreme Headquarters. This cannot, therefore, be called into question."[5]

American records bear out this French assertion. On April 1, 1949, three days before the signing of the North Atlantic Treaty, Secretary of State Acheson told Foreign Minister Schuman that

in effect, the new pact would add the U.S. and Canada to the Brussels Treaty. The arrangement should be such as to limit the real work of the Military Committee [of the North Atlantic Treaty] to four powers. Other devices could be worked out to ensure the association of the other countries as needed.[6]

On August 5, 1949, French and American senior military officers held a joint meeting in Paris to discuss the structures of the new pact, in anticipation of these being put in place definitively at the first meeting of the North Atlantic Council the following month. According to the official history of the American Joint Chiefs of Staff:

The JCS toured Western Europe during early August [1949] to ascertain the views of military authorities of the other members of NATO on military organization. They consulted the Chiefs of Staff of nine countries and discovered that only two of them, the British and the French, had given extensive consideration to the problems involved.[7]

In a meeting with their French counterparts on August 5, 1949, the representatives of the American Joint Chiefs of Staff presented four options regarding the military organization of the new alliance:

1. Plan A. A military committee composed of twelve members and presiding over two regional groups, one for Western Europe and the other called "Atlantic Ocean," made up of the United States and Canada.

2. Plan B. A military committee composed of twelve members but within it a small directing committee with a permanent headquarters, which would direct the activities of five regional groups: Canada—United States; Western Union; North Atlantic; Scandinavia; Western Mediterranean.

3. Plan C. A supreme command disposing of a headquarters with representatives of the twelve member states, under which would be four groups: Western Europe; Scandinavia; North Atlantic; Strategic Reserve.

4. Plan D. An Allied military council and an Allied headquarters in which the twelve signatory nations would be represented and which would have authority over seven regional groups: Canada and the United States; the Western European Chiefs of Staff (WUCOS); Italy; Portugal; Denmark; Norway; and Iceland.[8]

Only Plans A and B originated with the American Joint Chiefs of Staff (JCS). Plan C had been proposed by a European power. A French note of August 4, 1949, indicated that this was Britain.[9] This note further observed that Plan C "approached [that of an] operational organization in wartime and anticipates strategic arrangements for the defense of a space. It is in effect an organization of command and not an organization [of a] working group."[10]

As for Plan D, it was of political inspiration and aimed at serving the requirements of the smaller countries.[11]

The French officers liked Plan B. They agreed with Gen. Alfred Gruenther of the American delegation that the proposed Military Committee of the new pact would have to be retained, as it could not be eliminated in favor of a small directing committee. This was not acceptable to the smaller nations.[12]

Certain details remained to be worked out, such as whether to include Canada in the directing committee and the seat of the directing committee. Although the French were in favor of the inclusion of Canada (perhaps to de-Anglicize—somewhat—the directing committee), they readily agreed with Gen. Omar Bradley, who was about to become the first chairman of the Joint Chiefs of Staff, that if Canada were included, Italy would then ask to join. Gen. Georges Revers of the French delegation had initially taken the position that on the political level the French government was in favor of Canada's inclusion, and that this had been discussed between Foreign Minister Schuman and Secretary of State Acheson.[13] From the military point of view, said Revers, the French were neither requesting nor opposing membership for Canada.[14] As for the site of the directing committee, the French clearly preferred Washington.[15]

Another question was the relation of the new NATO structures to those of the Brussels Pact. In keeping with their desire to downgrade the Brussels Pact and, thereby, British hegemony, the French position was that the Brussels Pact should have no strategic role, only a military planning role.[16]

The question also remained of what to do with the Brussels Pact organs. It was obviously not politically feasible on either side of the Atlantic to do away with the Brussels Pact structures. The preferred French solution was to transfer the operational functions of the Brussels Pact structures to Washington, while retaining for the pact per se its planning functions:

The creation of the "Steering Group" and of the [Military] Committee of twelve military advisors will eventually involve the transfer of the operational functions of the WUCOS [Western Union Chiefs of Staff at Fontainebleau] to the organs at Washington. On the other hand, the WUCOS must retain entirely its mission of coordination and study, both for the submission of proposals to Washington, either collectively by the Five or individually by any one of the powers, and for the execution of decisions taken by the leading bodies of the Atlantic Pact.[17]

Under this concept, the Fontainebleau headquarters would become in effect the headquarters of the Regional Group for Western Europe, or, as a French staff note of August 2, 1949 put it, "The Fontainebleau Headquarters should be transformed [and should] become the Working Committee for the Western European Theater."[18] As for the Military Committee of the Brussels Pact, the same note of August 4 had this to say: "The Permanent Military Committee at London constitutes the military cell of the [Western] Union and the Headquarters of the Federal Army of the Five. In this capacity it has a role of coordination in terms of organization, mobilization, intelligence, training, equipment, and logistics, to the exclusion of any strategic function."[19]

WORKING OUT THE ATTRIBUTIONS OF THE STANDING GROUP

The first meeting of the NATO Council, set up under Article 9 of the Washington Treaty, was held on September 17, 1949, following preparation of proposals about structures put together by a working group. At this meeting, the council, which was made up of the foreign ministers of the member countries, essentially adopted Plan B advanced by the Joint Chiefs of Staff with their French counterparts at the August 5 meeting. The council set up a defense committee, as had been called for in Article 9 of the Treaty. This committee, made up of the defense ministers of the member countries, was charged with drawing up an overall defense plan for the North Atlantic area.[20]

Other entities created at this same meeting on September 17 were as follows:

- A Military Committee, composed of senior military representatives from each member country and charged with advising on military matters.
- A Standing Group, comprising one representative each from the United States, Britain, and France, to provide military information and guidance.
- Five Regional Planning Groups to prepare plans for the defense of each region (Northern Europe, Western Europe, Southern Europe, the Western Hemisphere, and the North Atlantic.[21]

The Standing Group was the new name for the Steering Committee, which did not include Canada. Thus, there finally came into being a "Directory of Three" (the United States, Great Britain, and France) but strictly within a military framework. The Standing Group sat in Washington, and the representatives on this body, though generals, were obviously not the highest-ranking military officers from their respective countries—otherwise, they would remain in their own capitals, certainly in peacetime. The first French representative on the Standing Group was Gen. Paul Ély.

And so, though the structures of the new pact conformed to Plan B, the above attribution of the Standing Group as that of providing military information and guidance was to fall considerably short of what the French desired. As Gen. Charles Lechères, one of the French representatives at the joint French-American meeting of August 5, stated in an exchange of views with General Bradley.

As a consequence of the Atlantic Pact, we envisage that subsequently, when we will have studied the strategic problems and defined the theaters of operation, it will be up to the Steering Committee [the Standing Group] to give operational directives to the theater commanders. We envisage this as a second stage. It is a difficult problem, but it is a problem we should logically solve.[22]

But this French attempt at collectivization of decision within the new alliance through the NATO Standing Group never really came about. The second stage envisaged by General Lechères ended quite differently for the French. While the structures established at the first North Atlantic Council meeting on September 17, 1949, resembled the JCS's Plan B, eventually NATO was to look more like Plan C, which, as was noted earlier, had been suggested by the British[23] and which, as was also noted,[24] was characterized by the French as more suited to a war footing: A year later, the creation of a supreme command, following the outbreak of the Korean War, was to have the effect of by-passing the Standing Group. In a sense, the French have been trying to get back to Plan B ever since.

As we have seen, it was the French intention that the Steering Committe (or Standing Group) would be the body that would give orders to the theater commanders.[25] While the creation of the Supreme Allied Commander Europe (SACEUR) did not change this hierarchy in principle, in practice the SACEUR was essentially independant of the Standing Group.

It is signficant in this regard that Charles de Gaulle, when he tried to establish a three-way strategic directorate (the United States, Great Britain, and France) upon his return to power in 1958, had not forgotten what the French saw as the inversion, in practice, of the original conception of the roles of the Standing Group and the SACEUR. De Gaulle concluded what came to be known as the Memorandum on the Directory with the following words:

The French Government suggests that the questions raised in this note be as soon as possible the subject of consultations between the United States, Great Britain, and France. It proposes that these consultations take place at Washington and, to begin with, through the medium of the Embassies and the Standing Group.[26]

To this day the French argue that, in real terms, there should be a higher body over the SACEUR. Since it can no longer be the Standing Group, which was abolished on July 1, 1966, because France left the NATO military organization, the French position is that the Military Committee of the Atlantic Pact should have real command over the SACEUR.

But at the time, in the critical years 1948–1950, the governments of the Fourth Republic were willing to sacrifice virtually anything in order to achieve a strategic parity with Great Britain. The Fontainebleau Headquarters, and Marshal Montgomery's presence there, was a symbol of this postwar lack of parity between the British and the French. As we have seen, the French were insistent that there be no strategic role for Fontainebleau; rather, this role should be transferred to Washington. Put another way, the French governments of the time opted for an American hegemony, which they did not contest. What they could not tolerate was subordination to the British.

Although the North Atlantic Treaty had been signed in April 1949, it had taken almost six months for the first council of the pact to be held and for the structures of the pact to be put in place. This delay was in part due to the Europeans' desire to have assurances beforehand of American military aid and to the delay in the legislation permitting this aid. The U.S. ratification of the pact did not take place until July, at which time the administration quickly introduced the initial legislation.

The U.S. Military Assistance Program (MAP) provided for $1,314,010,000, divided among three groups of countries: Title I (North Atlantic Pact countries), $1,000,000,000; Title II (Greece and Turkey), $211,370,000; and Title III (Iran, Korea, and the Philippines), $27,640,000. In addition, $75,000,000 was earmarked for the "general area" of China.[27] The authorization bill was finally signed into law by President Truman on October 6, 1949, under the name of the Mutual Defense Assistance Act of 1949.[28]

In anticipation of congressional cuts in the actual allocations of funds, however, the secretary of defense instructed the Joint Chiefs of Staff to adjust the figure downwards. The JCS proceeded to establish a limit of $900,000,000 for military equipment for Title I countries and $100,000,000 for industrial production in Western Europe. In the end, the allocations for military equipment for fiscal year 1950 totaled $891,500,000 for the NATO countries, of which France had by far the largest share ($556,560,000), and Great Britain, with $37,000,000, had the next-to-least ahead of Luxembourg. The allocations were based on an expected ground force of fourteen divisions for NATO: nine French, one Belgian, two Norwegian, and two Danish.[29]

The British figure was so low because these funds were allocated only to the Royal Air Force; in other words, nothing went to the army or navy. This was a result of the British refusal to commit themselves to provide troops for the defense of the Continent—even though Marshal Montgomery was presiding over the Western Union Chiefs of Staff Committee (WUCOS) at Fontainebleau!

Apart from Britain's "island mentality" and its traditional distaste for getting involved in Continental affairs, there were two contemporary reasons for this strange reluctance. First, there was the uncertainty over the American defense strategy. Was it to be focused on a "peripheral defense" of the Continent? In this case, a British troop commitment in Europe would be ill advised. Second, if Britain committed troops to Europe, it might not be able to cover its interests elsewhere, especially in the Middle East. Britain was a "global power"; and in the American optic of the time, France was not. According to an American account of a meeting between Foreign Secretary Bevin and Secretary of State Acheson in Washington on September 14, 1949,

Bevin . . . said he had been perturbed about our unwillingness to be members of the European regional groups. He would like us to be full partners in all their activities. . . . The French had tried to get the British to make specific commitments on their contribution of ground forces. The British feared being caught between pressure from the French for commitments in advance of or outside the grand plan and our unwillingness to furnish information on our own plans adequate to enable the British to make theirs. The British, like us, must pay due attention to global strategy.

Bevin . . . said that if Britain fully met the French desire for commitments on the continent, there would be no troops left for the Middle East. I [Acheson] said we could handle that between ourselves. He asked how much pressure the French had been exerting on us and was advised that the fact that the French were to be members of the Standing Group had temporarily reduced the pressure but that it would of course be renewed as soon as the organization began to function.[30]

On September 28, 1949, following the meeting of the North Atlantic Council setting up the Atlantic Pact structures, Evelyn Shuckburgh of the British Foreign Office told the American chargé d'affaires in London that his government was reassessing its attitude toward the construction of Europe. Among the factors that would bear on this was U.S. policy, particularly with respect to two points:

- the strength of the U.S. desire for unification of Europe and how far the U.S. really wished it to go.
- the extent that the United States was interested in seeing Great Britain involved on the Continent, particularly in view of the special relationship between Canada, the United States and Great Britain contemplated by the provision in the recent Washington talks for continued consultation.[31]

Although there is no further specific mention of these talks on a special relationship, it emerges from the file that this subject was discussed at a special Anglo-American working group meeting in Washington on September 7–12 to resolve the pressing problem of Britain's critical financial position.[32] Thus, at a moment when a sort of "supreme strategic body," the Standing Group, was being created at the first meeting of the North Atlantic Council on September 17, 1949, the "Anglo-Saxons" were proceeding along with their own kind of "special relationship" in strategic matters. In a way, the events surrounding the creation of the Atlantic Pact were a replay of those of a year and a half earlier, at the time of the Brussels Treaty. Hardly was the ink dry on the Brussels Pact, put together essentially between British and French negotiators, than the British were entering into separate "Anglo-Saxon" talks in Washington on global strategy.[33]

On January 5, 1950, a Strategic Defense Concept for NATO was signed, assigning initially to the United States strategic air operations; to the

United States and Great Britain the protection of the sea lanes of communications; and to the Continental powers of the pact the mission of defense by ground forces. On January 27, 1950, President Truman approved the Concept, and the way was cleared for completing the arrangements for the bilateral military aid pacts between the United States and the European members of NATO. The Congress had made release of the funding contingent on President Truman's approval of an integrated defense plan.[34]

THE GERMAN FACTOR

In this early period, 1948–1949, the Germans figured only peripherally in the strategic equation. The West German state was not even formed until November 1949. It was only from 1950 onwards that West Germany began to enter into the strategic calculations of the French. Though the French governments of the late 1940s did not entertain the idea of the Germans as a new strategic partner for the United States, they were concerned about the power represented by the reconstitution of Germany with U.S. financial help and what this would do to the position of the French as the primary land power of Western Europe. In the late 1940s, the main obsession of the French with the Germans was political and economic; it was the counterpart of the French obsession with British ascendancy in defense.

For General de Gaulle in 1945, the solution to the taming of Germany was to prevent the re-establishment of a centralized German state. De Gaulle, like most of his compatriots, was haunted by the memory of three German invasions within seventy years. Such could not be allowed to happen again. But in this case, the French, and virtually everyone else, could not visualize the great transformation that was to take place in German society at the end of the Second World War: A pervasive antimilitarist sentiment arose that has remained scarcely unchanged until this day.

The early leaders of the Fourth Republic were no more willing than General de Gaulle had been to raise the status of West Germany to that of a valid partner. The governments that followed de Gaulle stuck to this policy with great consistency, a consistency made easier because Georges Bidault remained foreign minister from November 1944 until July 1948. Although by autumn of 1947, French leaders had virtually lost all hope of a rapprochement with the Soviets, and through it an intermediary role for France between East and West, French policy toward Germany had scarcely changed. The leadership remained obsessed with Germany and particularly with the notion that Germany not be allowed to recover faster than France economically.

Bidault's departure from the Foreign Ministry in July 1948 was occasioned by a change of government in Paris. This change was largely attributed to backlash in France to the government's agreement, under Allied pressure, to merge its occupation zone with the other two Western zones, thus paving the way for the creation of the German Federal Republic. The agreement, reached in London and announced in a communiqué on June 7, 1948, was ratified by the French National Assembly only by a very narrow margin (300–286). Various factors contributed to such a high negative vote: anti-Germanism, fear of antagonizing the Soviets, and reluctance to be seen as following along with the Anglo-Americans. Naturally, the agreement was criticized by de Gaulle, whose newly formed political movement, the Rally of the French People (RFP), was still in the ascendancy. De Gaulle said several days before the vote: "The Government cannot and must not subscribe to the recommendations of the strange communiqué of London."[35]

A month later, on July 19, 1948, the Socialist ministers quit the government, and Prime Minister Schuman, who had been in office for nearly eight months, was forced to resign. However, Schuman became foreign minister in the following government, replacing Bidault. Thus began Schuman's long tenure in charge of the Quai d'Orsay that lasted virtually unbroken until the beginning of 1953.[36]

It was only after the departure of the unreconstructed nationalist Bidault and the emergence of the more European-minded Schuman as the man in charge of French foreign policy that France's intransigent attitude toward Germany started to change. Although as foreign minister Bidault had been associated with the London Accords that paved the way for the creation of a West German state, Bidault's position had remained to the end essentially that of an anti-German French nationalist. The evolution of French policy toward Germany began around the time of this change in the Foreign Ministry.[37] It was not a straight-line development, as there were many ups and downs to come, but it did lead to a fruitful relationship with Konrad Adenauer, the first chancellor of the Federal Republic, beginning with Robert Schuman and carried on by Charles de Gaulle.

Schuman had been born in Luxembourg. To escape German rule, his parents had moved to Luxembourg from the part of Lorraine that had been annexed after the Prussian victory in 1870. Schuman had even served in the German Army during World War I, since from the point of view of citizenship he still belonged to the German Empire. Schuman, interested in French-German reconciliation, but careful not to be seen as an advocate of a soft policy toward Germany, nevertheless aroused some suspicion in the French political class because of his Lorraine origins. The French Communist leader Jacques Duclos had even exclaimed, "Look at the Boche!" at one point when Schuman walked into the French National Assembly ("Boche" being the pejorative word used by the French for the Germans).

With the arrival at the Quai d'Orsay of the excessively calm and devoutly Catholic Schuman in place of the volatile and bibulous, though brilliant, Bidault, American diplomats found an interlocutor more to their liking. There was also on the part of Washington a growing impatience with British half-heartedness about a substantial troop commitment for the defense of the Continent.

Most senior American policymakers in this period (1949–1950) could see that France was the keystone arch in any defense system for Western Europe. This included some military figures such as Gen. Lauris Norstad. However, some American statesmen, in particular Dean Acheson, who became Secretary of State in January 1949, extended this perception to that of France assuming the leadership role in Western Europe. On October 19, 1949, in a message to a group of U.S. ambassadors meeting in Paris, Acheson noted that the integration of the countries of Western Europe had become an urgent necessity, due mainly to the evolution of the situation in West Germany. According to Acheson:

A dominant consideration underlying the belief that integration is needed is the problem of Western Germany. There are signs that [developments in Germany are] already taking a familiar and dangerous nationalist turn. This trend must be expected to continue unless German resources and energies can be harnessed to the security and welfare of Western Europe as a whole . . .

The key to progress toward integration is in French hands. In my opinion France needs, in the interests of her own future, to take the initiative promptly and decisively if the character of Western Germany is to be one permitting healthy development in Western Europe. Even with the closest possible relationship of the U.S. and the U.K. to the continent, France and France alone can take the decisive leadership in integrating Western Germany into Western Europe . . .

I believe that this may be the last chance for France to take the lead in developing a pattern of organization which is vital to her needs and to the needs of Western Europe . . . this . . . represent[s] our analysis of what is needed if Russian or German, or perhaps Russian-German domination is to be avoided.[38]

Acheson's reading of the situation was not met with unanimity by the ambassadors meeting in Paris. David Bruce, the American ambassador to Paris, considered it to be "unrealistic":

All of the nations that were defeated by Germany . . . are conscious of her latent power and are haunted by the fear that a reconstructed Germany will choose Russia rather than the West in the event of another war. This underlying factor . . . must be accepted as . . . basic . . . and compensated for as such. That is why the Department's telegram appears unrealistic in urging that France alone can take the lead in bringing about the reintegration of Germany into Western Europe. France, and indeed no continental power, can take that lead without assurances of the U.S. and the U.K. accompanied by precise and binding security commitments looking far into the future. We have been too tender with Britain since the

war: she has been the constant stumbling-block in the economic organization of
Europe . . .

We are therefore faced with the following proposition: economic integration of
Europe is impossible without the participation of the U.K.; upon it hinges the
reintegration of Germany into the Western community; such German reintegration
is a cardinal security necessity.[39]

With the creation of the West German state through the Petersberg
Accords of November 22, 1949, the French attitude toward this new entity
became critical. Though the French by this time had given up hopes of
any form of suzerainty over the Rhineland, the same was not true of their
designs over the Saar and the Ruhr. On March 3, 1950, France concluded
an agreement with authorities in the Saar, a provisions of which stated
that the Saar would be represented abroad by French diplomatic agents.
Konrad Adenauer, the new West German chancellor, promptly protested
these accords.

In the Ruhr, France, in November 1948, had protested an Anglo-
American plan to hand over management of the Ruhr's coal and steel
production to German authorities. In the face of the French protest, the
United States and Great Britain agreed to create an international authority for the Ruhr made up of representatives of the three Western occupying powers. This authority, set up on April 28, 1949, was accepted by
the Germans in the Petersberg Accords of seven months later, which set
forth the relationship between the West German state and the three Western occupying powers.

In the spring of 1950, relations between France and the new West
German state were highly tentative. Despite a visit by Schuman to Bonn
in January of that year for meetings with Konrad Adenauer, the French
hold over the Saar, which could never be accepted by the Germans, remained a major obstacle to normalization of relations.

The breakthrough came in the other principal area of contention, the
Ruhr. Although the idea of pooling France's and Germany's coal and steel
resources had been in the air for some time, French officials, led by Jean
Monnet, who had been the government's planning and development commissioner since the beginning of 1946, now suggested a revolutionary approach: to take these resources out from under the two governments and
place coal and steel production in the hands of an authority that would
be above and apart—what became known in the vocabulary of the time
as a *supranational* authority.

The merging of the coal and steel resources of the Ruhr Valley and
Lorraine was not only for economic reasons but was also a political move
to ensure that Germany and France would become linked together economically and would not go to war again. Theoretically, with this major
war-making potential removed from their direct control, the two

governments would be prevented from making war against each other. The chief cause of Europe's instability in the last half of the nineteenth century and the first half of the twentieth—German-French hostility— would be reduced if not eliminated.

Monnet, encouraged by the prospect of German receptivity, as evidenced in a speech by Konrad Adenauer on March 9, 1950, put his ideas into a draft with the help of his colleague Paul Reuter. Monnet then proceeded to interest Schuman's cabinet director, Bernard Clappier, in the project. Another Monnet aide, Etienne Hirsch, worked over the draft, which went through nine versions before it was in a form acceptable to Monnet. Clappier gave it to Schuman who took it to his weekend retreat in Lorraine.

At this point, Schuman was under some pressure from his Anglo-American counterparts to come up with a more positive French policy toward West Germany. On May 10, 1950, Schuman was due to meet in London with Secretary of State Acheson and Foreign Secretary Bevin to discuss this subject. Upon his return to Paris from Lorraine on May 1, Schuman informed Clappier, "I've read the paper of Monnet and the answer is yes."[40]

Schuman made only a vague mention of Monnet's idea at a Cabinet meeting on May 3 but planned to make a full exposition of the plan at the next meeting on May 9. In the meantime, Schuman sent one of his aides, Robert Mischlich, to Bonn on May 8 to take the plan to Konrad Adenauer. Mischlich, who met Adenauer on the morning of May 9, also delivered a personal message from Schuman. Adenauer, overwhelmed, readily agreed to the plan: "This proposition of France, historic in all respects, which renders to my country its dignity, is also the cornerstone of the unity of Europe, in which I believe more than ever."[41]

Mischlich immediately telephoned the word to Clappier. The latter interrupted a Cabinet meeting in which Schuman was explaining the plan in detail for the first time, running up against the objections of the prime minister, Georges Bidault, and the silence of a surprised Vincent Auriol.[42] It appears that Bidault had been given some idea of the project prior to the May 9 Cabinet meeting but did not focus on the matter before that point.[43] When Clappier brought in the news of Adenauer's approval, this helped carry the day, and the objections were withdrawn.

With Cabinet approval in hand, the principal European ambassadors in Paris were immediately informed and then the press was given a briefing later on the same afternoon. By that evening, May 9, the Benelux countries had given their assent to joining the plan, which was to become known as the European Coal and Steel Community (ECSC). Schuman was due to fly to London the following day to meet with the British and American foreign ministers to discuss policy toward Germany. Indeed, Schuman had managed to advance the Cabinet meeting by one day in order to ensure that the coal and steel project would have been set in motion by the time he arrived in London to meet with his two allied counterparts.

Though the British were invited to join the coal and steel project, it was essential in Monnet's view that the centerpiece of the plan be laid in place first: the acceptance in principle of the pooling by France and Germany of their war-making recources, so that they would not engage in further conflicts against each other.[44]

Neither Schuman, nor Monnet who followed him to London, were able to convince the British to join the coal and steel project. By nature reluctant to cede any national prerogatives to a "supranational "High Authority" (in this case over coal and steel), the British were also stung by the French failure to inform them beforehand. "Something has changed between our two countries," an annoyed Foreign Minister Bevin observed to French Ambassador Rene Massigli when the latter on May 9 informed him unofficially about the Schuman Plan.[45]

It is not surprising that the one great French foreign policy accomplishment during this period from 1945 to 1951—the European Coal and Steel Community—was the product of secret diplomacy. Because it went against the grain of the prevailing French attitudes toward Germany, it had to be accomplished without fanfare; in short, by the "Monnet method"—working behind the scenes through a wide network of contacts; using a pragmatic, step-by-step approach wedded to the accomplishment of an overall vision; and being able to convince people to work together. By his own account, Monnet's aim in life was "to unite men, to solve the problems that divide them, and to persuade them to see their common interest."[46]

NOTES

1. *Service Historique de l'Armée de Terre* (SHAT), General Secretariat of National Defense (SGDN), Affaires générales, NATO, Dossier 6Q7242, meeting of French and American General Staff Chiefs, 1949, note dated August 2, 1949, and entitled "The French Thesis on the Military Organization of the Atlantic Pact," 4.

2. Ibid., note of June 10, 1949, 1.

3. Ibid., note of August 23, 1949, 8.

4. Ibid., note of June 10, 1949, 1–2.

5. Ibid., note of August 2, 1949, 3.

6. *Foreign Relations of the United States* (FRUS) (1949), vol. 4, *Western Europe* (Washington, D.C.: Government Printing Office, 1975), 266.

7. Kenneth W. Condit, *The History of the Joint Chiefs of Staff: The Joint Chiefs of Staff and National Policy* (Wilmington: Michael Glazier, 1979), 2:389.

8. SHAT, SGDN, minutes of meeting of August 5, 1949, 2–5.

9. Ibid., note preliminary to the August 5 meeting, 2.

10. Ibid.

11. Ibid., minutes of the August 5 meeting, 4.

12. Ibid., 5.

13. This was at their meeting on April 1, 1949, three days prior to the signing of the North Atlantic Treaty. See p. 76, this chapter.

14. SHAT, SGDN, minutes of meeting of August 5, 1949, part 2, 6.

15. Ibid.

16. Ibid., note of August 2, 1949, 3.

17. Ibid., Personal and Secret Directive for the French Military Representative at the Forthcoming Meetings in Washington, August 23, 1949, 2–3.

18. Ibid., note of August 2, 1949, 3.

19. Ibid.

20. Henry W. Degenhardt, ed., *Treaties and Alliances of the World* (Detroit: Gale Research, 1986), 209. (In May 1951, the Defense Committee ceased to exist as a separate body and was incorporated in the North Atlantic Council, which became the sole ministerial body of NATO [Ibid].)

21. Ibid.

22. SHAT, SGDN, minutes of meeting of August 5, 1949, part 2, 11–12.

23. See p. 77, this chapter.

24. See p. 77, this chapter.

25. See p. 79, this chapter.

26. *Dwight D. Eisenhower Presidential Library* (DDEL), Documents of DDE-President (Ann Whitman File), International Series, Box 11, France 1956–1960, Letter from de Gaulle to Eisenhower (known as the "Memorandum on the Directory") September 17, 1958, 3.

27. Condit, *History of the JCS*, 2:433. (At that time the fiscal year began on July 1 of the previous year and ended on June 30 of the named year. The cycle is now moved forward three months to begin on October 1.)

28. FRUS (1949), 4:341.

29. Condit, *History of the JCS*, 2:433–36.

30. FRUS (1949), 4:325–26. N.B. "European regional groups" referred to are the five regional planning groups contemplated within the NATO structure. See p. 79, this chapter. At that time, the United States, and specifically the Joint Chiefs of Staff, were unwilling to go beyond the formula that the United States would "participate as appropriate" in these planning groups (Ibid., 326).

31. Ibid., 339–40.

32. Ibid., 832 ff.

33. See pp. 45 ff, Chapter 3.

34. Doris M. Condit, *History of the Office of the Secretary of Defense, vol. 2, The Test of War, 1950–1953* (Washington, D.C.: Historical Office, Office of the Secretary of Defense, 1988), 311.

35. "Chronologie: Charles de Gaulle et son temps," in Charles de Gaulle, *Le Fil de l'Épée* (Paris: Éditions Berger-Levrault, 1944), entry for June 9, 1948.

36. Robert Mischlich, *Une mission secrète à Bonn* (Lausanne, Switzerland: Fondation Jean Monnet pour l'Europe et Centre de recherches européennes, 1986), 25.

37. Stanley Hoffman, conversation with author, March 13, 1996.

38. FRUS (1949) 4:469–72.

39. Ibid., 492–93.

40. Mischlich, *Mission secrète*, 55.

41. Ibid., 61.

42. François Fontaine, "La naissance de la Communauté européenne," *Le Monde*, May 6–7 1990, 2.

43. Mischlich, *Mission secrète*, 55.

44. Jean Monnet, *Memoirs* (Garden City, N.Y.: Doubleday, 1978), 306, 336.

45. Ibid., 305.

46. Ibid., 221.

CHAPTER 6

NATO Produces an Integrated Command

HEIGHTENED THREAT FROM THE SOVIET UNION

The Soviet ending of the Berlin blockade in May 1949 and the convening of a new Conference of Foreign Ministers (CFM) in yet another attempt to solve the German problem seemed for a moment to bring a certain relaxation in East-West tensions. The interlude was short lived. The CFM ended inconclusively in June, and the three Western allies proceeded to establish a West German state in September, with Konrad Adenauer as chancellor. The Soviets responded the following month with the creation of a state in East Germany, with Wilhelm Pieck as president.

In addition to this definitive break with the Soviets over Germany, three events took place in late 1949 and in 1950 that produced a greatly heightened sense of urgency concerning the defense of Europe.

The first was the explosion of the first Soviet atomic bomb in August 1949. The second was the triumph of the Communists in mainland China in October 1949. The third was the invasion of South Korea in June 1950.

On October 17, 1949, the U.S. delegation to the Military Committee of the Western Union produced a staff study on the effect of Soviet possession of the atomic bomb on Western Union planning. According to the findings of this study, the Soviet Union would eventually have the means to deliver a powerful and possibly decisive blow to the West—but not until it had developed an effective stockpile. The study estimated that in three to five years, the Soviets would have an adequate stockpile and thus would be able to engage in an all-out war. However, though the Soviet position had been strengthened militarily and politically by possession of the bomb, the Western Union's basic strategy should remain unchanged.

Nevertheless, the Western Union powers should consider how to increase their most urgent means of production, in order to offset the Soviet gains.[1] Consequently, Western planners set a target date of July 1, 1954, for a state of NATO readiness such as to challenge effectively any Soviet military move in Europe.

Two events spurred a review within the U.S. government as to the implications for the West: the Soviet atomic explosion and the Communist victory in China, both taking place within two months of each other. Sponsored by the State Department's Policy Planning Staff and its new chief, Paul Nitze, who had succeeded George Kennan, the study, which emerged in April 1950 as NSC-68, became the document that defined U.S. strategy for the Cold War. It was, in effect, an operationalization of Kennan's advocacy of "containment" for the Soviet Union, which was embodied in the latter's "long telegram" of November 1946 from Moscow and was published in an unclassified version in *Foreign Affairs* of July 1947, under the pseudonym "X." But this operationalization stopped short of advocating direct conflict. NSC-68 mandated "intensification of affirmative and timely measures and operations by covert means in the fields of economic warfare and political and psychological warfare with a view to fomenting and supporting unrest and revolt in selected strategic satellite countries."[2]

The first Soviet atomic explosion, which had taken place two years earlier than anticipated, was in effect an existential event; the immanent danger had increased but was still not tangible. It was the North Korean invasion of South Korea on June 25, 1950, that produced the shock that woke up the West to the danger in Europe. It seemed to fulfill the warnings of NSC-68, as Kathryn Weathersby pointed out:

NSC-68 argued that if the United States failed to move decisively to counter future Soviet aggression, U.S. allies in Western Europe would lose heart and drift into a dangerous neutrality. The report warned that any American failure to respond to Soviet aggression, which would more likely be "piecemeal" than total war, could lead to "a descending spiral of too little and too late . . . of even narrower and more desperate alternatives . . . of gradual withdrawals under pressure until we discover one day that we have sacrificed positions of vital interest."

From the perspective of the schematic thinking represented in NSC-68, the sudden, massive assault on the American client state in South Korea by the armed forces of the Soviet client state in North Korea clearly constituted a challenge the United State must answer.[3]

Theretofore, though the threat of a Communist armed attack was always latent, it had nevertheless not taken place. Now it was suddenly real. As recounted in the *History of the Joint Chiefs of Staff*, "Overt Soviet attack, once an improbable hypothesis, now seemed a menacing possibility. . . . Indeed, Western impotence created acute political and psychological problems among Europeans, generating what State Department analysts termed a 'fear and resignation psychosis' which threatened to erode the alliance's 'moral tissue.' "[4]

The surprise attack by North Korea led to widespread speculation that a similar proxy war launched by East Germany against West Germany could be in the offing. It was not known at the time whether the Soviets had ordered, or acquiesced in, the attack. We now know that the latter was the case. According to a classified internal history of the Korean War written by the staff of the Soviet Foreign Ministry,

Calculating that the USA would not enter a war over South Korea, Kim Il Sung persistently pressed for agreement from Stalin and Mao Zedong to reunify the country by military means.

Stalin at first treated the persistent appeals of Kim Il Sung with reserve ... but he did not object in principle. The final agreement to support the plans of the Koreans was given by Stalin at the time of Kim Il Sung's visit to Moscow in March–April 1950. Following this, in May, Kim Il Sung visited Beijing and secured the support of Mao.[5]

The new uncertainty over Soviet intentions reflected by the events in Korea, which was magnified greatly with the Chinese armed attack across the Yalu River in November, called for an urgent reappraisal of the strategy of the North Atlantic Alliance. Coming at a moment when France's attitude toward Germany was beginning to soften, as we have seen in the previous chapter, the reappraisal focused on two ways to overcome Western weakness: (1) put German troops into the equation on the Western side; and (2) streamline the cumbersome command arrangements of NATO by appointing a sole commander in charge of the defense of the West.

JOINT CHIEFS OF STAFF PRESS FOR GERMAN REARMAMENT

Even before the North Korean invasion, the American Joint Chiefs of Staff had declared themselves, in a memorandum on May 2, 1950, "firmly of the opinion that, from the military point of view, the appropriate and early rearming of Western Germany is of fundamental importance to the successful defense of Western Europe against the USSR." Germany should be given "real and substantial opportunity to participate in Western European and North Atlantic defense arrangements." In particular, France must be "persuaded to recognize that the USSR is a greater menace to [its] independence ... than is Germany."[6]

Although the outbreak of the Korean War added a new urgency to the German troop issue, the State Department, in a memorandum on July 3,

1950, disagreed with the JCS position. The State paper argued that the softening French attitude toward Germany might be completely reversed by precipitate U.S. action. The State Department considered it premature for the United States "publicly to advocate or otherwise press for action in the question of the establishment of German armed forces."[7]

On July 31, 1950, Secretary of State Acheson explored with President Truman means to overcome the dilemma of making use of German military manpower without antagonizing the Europeans, especially the French. In Acheson's account, they were looking for "some way of merging Germany's military contribution into a European Army or North Atlantic Army with an integrated command and, perhaps, supply. The latter could move German industry further into a European system already started by the Schuman Plan."[8]

The integrated command to which Acheson referred reflected an increased perception that NATO's command arrangements—described as "absolutely hopeless" in a meeting of Acheson, Secretary of Defense Louis Johnson, and Ambassador Averill Harriman on August 3, 1950[9]—had to be improved. As things stood at that moment, political and military control over NATO was exercised on a day-to-day basis respectively by two permanent bodies: the Committee of Deputies of the North Atlantic Council and the Standing Group of the Military Committee. The former, which could only act on a subject when so empowered by the council, was based in London; the latter was based in Washington. The Standing Group found it very difficult to establish any continuity of authority over the Regional Planning Groups located in Europe. For this reason, a centralized (or "integrated," in the vocabulary of the time) command in Europe was seen as an evident necessity.

At this point, as the NATO partners were preparing for a decisive meeting of the North Atlantic Council in September 1950, the U.S. Defense Department came up with what was called a "one package" approach: the United States would withhold setting up a unified command and would withhold sending additional American troop reinforcements to Europe until the Europeans agreed to German rearmament. Acheson, while finding the objective laudable, described the tactics as "murderous." In Acheson's view, it was much better to go at the problem a different way: "Once we established the unified command and had a planning center, the inevitable logic of mathematics would convince everyone that any plan without Germany was untenable."[10]

A key flaw in the hard-headed approach of the Defense Department was that unless there were a significant presence of American troops in Western Europe, it would be very difficult to convince the West Germans to take up arms against the Russian threat. Thus, the creation of a unified (or integrated) command, including a planning staff, would not be sufficient in itself for this purpose. A larger commitment of American troops would be necessary to boost European, including German, morale.

THE FRENCH PRESS FOR A UNIFIED NATO COMMAND

In the meantime, the French reacted to the new pressures on them caused by the Korean War by eluding the question of German rearmament. Instead, they concentrated on improving NATO's existing structures. In two notes to Washington on August 5 and 17, 1950, Paris advocated (1) more financial aid to the United States for NATO; (2) greater ground force participation by other NATO members; and (3) the creation of a unified command for NATO.[11] The French visualized this unified command as centered on the Standing Group, which would become in effect NATO's General Staff:

In the military field, the Atlantic nations must move quickly toward unity of command. Plans must be made for the constitution of an agency . . . like the combined chiefs of staff in the last war. . . . The French Government thinks that for this purpose the permanent group should henceforth function as a general staff. It would thus be in a position to become the organ of the High Command of all possible theaters of operation. . . . Every [theater] would be placed under one command with a general staff which would be subordinated to the permanent group The present regional so-called "planning" groups would thus be eliminated. . . .

All the agencies, whether established under the Brussels Pact or the Atlantic Pact, which are at present duplicating work should also be eliminated.[12]

Thus, the French were at that point finessing the question of German rearmament. In this, they were operating from a strong hand, based in part on the fact that the sole existing *European* security organization, the Western Union, did not include Germany. Nor were the Germans members of NATO, and few if any outside the American Joint Chiefs of Staff were suggesting that they should be. At the same time, the French were responding to the pressures generated by the North Korean attack in opening the door for the creation of a unified command and, more generally, for a militarization of the Atlantic Alliance.

American planners had a different view of the purposes behind a unified command than did the French, as evidenced by the Acheson statement already quoted.[13] For the Americans, the unified command—with a sole effective commander—would have charge over a European defense force that would include German units. For the French, the unified command, at the pinnacle of which would be the Standing Group, would have control over NATO forces that would not include Germans.

The "one package" plan—in other words, an insistence on the part of

the Americans to proceed with German rearmament—fell apart in the
protracted North Atlantic Council (NAC) meeting in New York, which
began on September 12, 1950. Acheson, who by now had agreed to the
"one package" plan, described the discussions in the following terms:

Frustrating and inconclusive as they seemed at the time, they comprised the first
real debate NATO had had about the twin subjects of Germany and European
defense. . . . [At an earlier meeting] in May we had talked long and earnestly but
about abstractions and phrases. In September we closed with fact and brutal com-
parisons of aims and capabilities.[14]

In the September NAC meeting, the French agreed to the idea of a
unified command but balked on the issue of German rearmament. Defense
Minister Jules Moch, who represented France in the later stages of the
meeting (and whose son had been killed in World War II), was later to
describe the American linkage of the unified command with German rearmament as in effect a breach of faith.[15]

In a preliminary communiqué, issued on September 19 at the start of a
three-day recess, the NATO ministers took a position against the creation
of a German national army but agreed, however, to increase their own
forces in Germany and to "treat any attack against the Federal Republic
or Berlin from any quarter as an attack upon themselves."[16]

The NAC's final communiqué, issued on September 26, approved the
creation of an integrated force of the member nations to defend Western
Europe, which comprised West Germany as well. A supreme commander
would be appointed as soon as adequate national forces had been assembled. The Standing Group would be the superior military body to which
the supreme commander would be responsible.[17] Pending the appointment
of a supreme commander, a chief of staff would be named provisionally.[18]

The NAC left vague the issue of German rearmament, though the principle had been admitted. The council directed the Defense Committee to
come up with specific recommendations as to how Germany could make
a contribution, "bearing in mind the unanimous conclusion of the Council
that it would not serve the best interests of Europe or Germany to bring
into being a German national army or a German general staff."[19]

Further decisions on German rearmament were deferred until a meeting
of the NATO defense ministers in late October.[20] This meeting would be
preceded by successive bilateral French-American and British-American
talks in Washington.

THE FRENCH COME UP WITH THE PLEVEN PLAN FOR
THE USE OF GERMAN TROOPS

The French, finding themselves essentially alone in resisting German
rearmament, struggled to come up with an alternate proposal. Once again,

Jean Monnet entered the picture, but this time less felicitously. Initially, American policymakers had gotten the impression that France would seek to apply the principles of the European Coal and Steel Community (ECSC) to the creation of a new European Army.[21] Though this was Monnet's general idea, the proposal, which came to be known as the Pleven Plan, took on quite a different hue. The plan, as presented to the French National Assembly by Prime Minister René Pleven on October 24, 1950, four days prior to the convening of the NATO Defense Committee, violated the ECSC principle of equal treatment for West Germany. This was a principle that had been insisted upon by Konrad Adenauer, both with respect to the ECSC and to German rearmament:

My precondition for German participation in European defense was complete equality between Germany and the other European nations. . . . Rearmament might be the way to gaining full sovereignty for the Federal Republic. . . . The Western Allies, especially France, had to be made to answer the question of which danger was the greater: the Russian threat or a German contribution to a European defense community.[22]

Although the American position, as expressed by the Joint Chiefs of Staff, was that German ground troops should join NATO forces on a national basis and that Germany should be made a member of NATO,[23] the Pleven Plan contained nothing of the sort. As reported by Ambassador David Bruce in Paris on October 23 and as presented to the NATO defense ministers by Jules Moch four days later in Washington, there was to be no German membership in either the Western Union or NATO, no German national army, no German general staff, but only German troops, and these in formations no larger than battalions.

The Pleven Plan as initially spelled out by Moch even contained the idea that training and leadership would be provided by French cadres for the German elements in the European army—an army that would eventually grow to 100,000 men. As elements became effective, they would be placed under the Supreme Commander.[24] Other national contingents would also join the European Army, and a defense minister for the ensemble would be named by the governments adhering to the plan.[25]

The European Army, as proposed by Jean Monnet to Prime Minister Pleven in October 1950, was to be under a supranational authority, to which the defense minister for Europe, named by the participating governments, would be responsible. This supranational authority in the defense area would develop progressively and in parallel with the Coal and Steel Community.[26]

Strictly speaking, it was not logical for the European Army to be a part of NATO because the Germans in it were not to be members of NATO. And yet, the European Army was to be ultimately under the command of the NATO Supreme Commander. This strange hybrid was rationalized as follows by Pleven, in his October 24 speech to the French National Assembly in which he presented his plan: "Germany, which is not part of the Atlantic Pact, is nevertheless going to benefit from the security system that results from it. It is therefore right that she should furnish her contribution."[27]

British and American leaders were variously skeptical or aghast at the Pleven Plan as it was originally presented. As recorded in the *History of the Joint Chiefs of Staff*:

Secretary Acheson . . . adjudged the scheme "hopeless"; General Marshall professed inability to penetrate the plan's "miasma." UK Defense Minister Shinwell privately denounced the proposal as "disgusting and nauseous . . . military folly and political madness." Indeed, he averred that the plan was consciously devised to be unacceptable, thereby offering a means of escape from France's NATO obligations.[28]

Perhaps the most telling criticism of all was that of General Omar Bradley, chairman of the Joint Chiefs of Staff: "This organization of a Minister of Defense of Europe cuts across practically all the lines of NATO and, if adopted, would make NATO impossible."[29]

However, Bradley's fears turned out to be unfounded: A bifurcation was to take place between the Coal and Steel Community, on the one hand, and the Pleven Plan (later to become known as the European Defense Community), on the other, The Coal and Steel Community would retain its character as a purely European entity run by a supranational community or authority. The European Defense Community, had it come into being, would have been quite different: While retaining its communitarian trappings—a high authority, an assembly, and even a court—it would in real terms have come under the command of NATO, in the person of the Supreme Commander.

There were two other fatal flaws in the Pleven Plan. First, national defense was far different than coal and steel and surrender of even partial sovereignty in defense to a supranational authority was too much for French national pride. Second, the formula of the exclusion of Britain, which had worked so well in getting the Coal and Steel Community started, backfired when it was applied to the defense community. It meant, in effect, that, of the two oldest nations of Europe, one had to surrender some of its sovereignty over defense (France) and the other did not (Britain).

Monnet, after starting out on a small scale, and with a long-term vision in mind, this time applied the same principle of supranationality to a problem of the moment: the need of German soldiers for the defense of the West. In stepping out of the realm of coal and steel and into the highly sensitive area of defense, Monnet overreached himself. Although his powers of persuasion were such that the French Cabinet adopted his proposal in favor of a European Defense Community and thus of German rearmament, this went far more against the grain of the French people than did the Coal and Steel Community. As General de Gaulle, who opposed both the Coal and Steel Community and the Defense Community, put it with regard to the latter: "Of course France, among all the great nations which today have an army, is the only one to lose hers."[30]

The NATO Defense Committee meeting (October 28–31) ended without a decision because all the ministers except the French (Jules Moch) were opposed to the Pleven plan. However, the Chinese intervention in Korea the next month greatly increased the pressure for action in the defense of Europe. In a special summit between U.S. President Truman and British Prime Minister Attlee in early December, it was agreed that the most urgent step needed to shore up the Western position in Europe was to name a supreme commander without delay.[31]

The impasse over German rearmament was broken in a joint meeting of the North Atlantic Council and the Defense Committee on December 18–19, 1950, in Brussels—a meeting held in an atmosphere inflamed by the fear of another world war.[32] An accord was reached for an integrated defense force under a centralized command.[33] The United States backed away from its insistence that German elements entering the European Defense Force on a national basis be no smaller than division level. Although the principle of division level was not disavowed, it was agreed that the level of regimental combat teams would be acceptable if necessary for political reasons.[34]

Other concessions to European fears were also made, notably the restriction of the German troop element to 20 percent of the total. Two-track negotiations were to begin: one between the Allied High Commissioners and the Germans, on the question of how the German units were to be formed; and the other among the six governments of the Coal and Steel Community, to discuss the concept of a European Defense Force. The principle of forming this force was accepted, provided that it did not retard the process of German rearmament.[35]

The NAC, having approved these steps, which had been recommended jointly by the Military Committee and the council's Deputies Committee,[36] proceeded to call for the naming of a supreme commander. Acheson suggested that this be done without delay. Jules Moch agreed that this was the time for action and suggested the name he thought was in the minds of everybody: Gen. Dwight D. Eisenhower.[37] The next day, December 19, on the final day of the NAC meeting, Eisenhower was named Supreme Commander.

The French government had given way only partially on German rearmament. Much negotiation remained to be done. But it had willingly

allowed itself to be swept along by the idea of Eisenhower as Supreme
Commander for Europe. The way to NATO's integrated command, which
was to become the Gaullist bugbear of the 1950s and 1960s, had now been
opened.

NOTES

1. *National Archives II* (NA II) Joint Chiefs of Staff (JCS) Geographic Files,
1948–1950, Box 97, Western Europe (3–12–48), Section 32.

2. Ernest R. May, ed. and intro., *American Cold War Strategy: Interpreting
NSC 68* (Boston: Bedford Books of St. Martin's Press, 1993), 74.

3. Kathryn Weathersby, "Soviet Aims in Korea and the Origins of the Korean
War: New Evidence from Russian Archives," Working Paper no. 8, *Cold War
International History Project* (Washington, D.C.: Woodrow Wilson Center, 1993),
2.

4. NA II, Walter Poole, *The History of the Joint Chiefs of Staff: The Joint
Chiefs of Staff and National Policy*, vol. 4, 1950–1952, 186.

5. Weathersby, "Soviet Aims in Korea," 24.

6. NA II, Poole, *History of the JCS*, 4:192 (JCS memo to secretary of defense,
May 2, 1950).

7. Ibid., 193 (State memo of July 3, 1950).

8. Dean Acheson, *Present at the Creation* (New York: W. W. Norton, 1969),
437. (Cited in NA II, Poole, *History of the JCS*, 4:194.)

9. *Foreign Relations of the United States* (FRUS) (1950), vol. 3 *Western Europe*
(Washington, D.C.: Government Printing Office, 1977), 182–83. (Cited in NA II,
Poole, *History of the JCS*, 4:194–95.)

10. Acheson, *Present at the Creation*, 438. (Cited in NA II, Poole, *History of the
JCS*, 4:195.)

11. NA II, Poole, *History of the JCS*, 4:196.

12. FRUS (1950), 3:221–22. (French note of August 17.) N.B. "Permanent
Group" is the way the French designated the Standing Group of NATO.

13. See p. 94, this chapter.

14. Acheson, *Present at the Creation*, 443. (Cited in NA II, Poole, *History of the
JCS*, 4:203.)

15. FRUS (1950), 3:427. (Cited in NA II, Poole, *History of the JCS*, 4:213.)

16. NA II, Poole, *History of the JCS*, 4:204.

17. Ibid., 206.

18. *Informations Militaires* no. 161 (1950):3.

19. NA II, Poole, *History of the JCS*, 4:207.

20. *Informations Militaires* no. 161 (1950):3.

21. NA II, Poole, *History of the JCS*, 4:211. (Memorandum of a conversation
on October 11, 1950, among Acheson, Defense Secretary Marshall, and the latter's
deputy Robert Lovett).

22. Konrad Adenauer, *Memoirs: 1945–1953*, trans. Beate Ruhm von Oppen
(Chicago: Henry Regnery, 1966), 270. (Cited in NA II, Poole, *History of the JCS*,
4:195.)

23. NA II, Poole, *History of the JCS*, 4:199. Also see p. 93, this chapter.

24. Ibid., 211–12. (Sourced to Paris 2192 to State, October 23, 1950: to Memo of Conversation, "Inclusion of Germany in an Integrated Force, dated October 27, 1950, CCS 092 Western Europe, 3–12–48, section 62; and to Acheson, *Present at the Creation*, 458.) N.B. The idea of French cadres for German troops was subsequently withdrawn.

25. *Informations Militaires* no. 163 (1950):5.

26. Georgette Elgey, *La République des illusions* (Paris: Fayard, 1965), 1:462.

27. *Le Monde*, August 20–21, 1989, 2.

28. NA II, Poole, *History of the JCS*, 4:212.

29. Ibid.

30. Charles de Gaulle, *Discours et Messages, vol. II, Dans l'attente, Février 1946– Avril 1958* (Paris: Plon, 1970), 524.

31. NA II, Poole, *History of the JCS*, 4:216–217.

32. Ibid., 218.

33. Henry W. Degenhardt, ed., *Treaties and Alliances of the World* (Detroit, MI: Gage Research, 1986), 209.

34. FRUS (1950), 3:542.

35. NA II, Poole, *History of the JCS*, 4:219.

36. Ibid., 218.

37. FRUS (1950), 3:591.

CHAPTER 7

The Return of the Supreme Commander

On January 1, 1951, General Eisenhower returned to Europe. He began his assignment as Supreme Commander Allied Forces Europe (SACEUR)—a job that had been offered to him in October 1950 by President Truman—with a trip to eleven of the twelve NATO capitals (the exception being Iceland). In May 1951, he moved into the Supreme Headquarters, Allied Powers Europe (SHAPE), set up at Rocquencourt, outside Paris in the Versailles region.

Eisenhower's return was in a sense a remake of the wartime experience. It was but a leap, conceptually, from the Supreme Headquarters Allied Expeditionary Force (SHAEF) of World War II to the Supreme Headquarters Allied Powers Europe. In fact, the SACEUR/SHAPE system was consciously drawn from the wartime precedent. At the NAC meeting in September 1950, as noted in the previous chapter, it was agreed to create the position of Chief of Staff to the Supreme Allied Commander (COSSAC) forthwith, and prior to the actual naming of a supreme commander. This decision was based on a recommendation that had been made by the American Joint Chiefs of Staff to the Standing Group: namely, that an organization be created consisting of a "Chief of Staff and his staff of certain NATO forces in Europe."[1] This procedure was to follow the earlier wartime example:

In general, the Chief of Staff's position would parallel that filled by COSSAC in 1943, prior to General Eisenhower's appointment as Supreme Commander Allied Expeditionary Forces. Acting Chief of Staff to an unknown Supreme Commander, Lieutenant General Frederick Morgan of Great Britain had assembled a headquarters staff and conducted preliminary planning for the cross-channel assault.[2]

In this case, however, the Supreme Commander position was filled before that of COSSAC, even though the NAC had directed that the appointment to the former position be withheld until sufficient national forces had been committed.[3]

The reason for Eisenhower's return—the cold war—as the Supreme Commander in Europe served to reinforce the parallel with his World War II role and thereby to increase his authority. Eisenhower was obviously conscious of the parallel and of the continuity in his mission. As Stephen E. Ambrose wrote, "Best of all, he would be in a position to preserve the victory he had directed in 1945."[4] To his boyhood confidant, "Swede" Hazlett, Eisenhower said before his departure, "I rather look upon this effort as about the last remaining chance for the survival of Western civilization."[5]

Not everyone in Europe, and especially in France, agreed with this appraisal. According to Georgette Elgey, "Upon his arrival in Paris in January 1951, [Eisenhower] was struck, not by demonstrations of hostility against him, but rather by the lack of demonstrations of friendship. He deduced from this that the United States was not very popular in France."[6]

THE FRENCH POSTWAR MALAISE

The postwar mood of France was one of morosity and creativity. At the same time as Paris had become the center of Europe's postwar intellectual renaissance, it is striking how, in the late 1940s, many French leaders believed that a third world war was imminent. De Gaulle's writings reveal this. Already, in November 1945, he had written to a friend, "Don't you think that we're already between two wars?"[7] A year later, after he had left the government, he told two leaders of the *Mouvement Républicain Populaire*, who had come to visit him at his retreat at Colombey-les-Deux-Églises, "We have just ended the second round. And the war continues. The third round is inevitable. The confrontation with the Soviets is much closer than people think."[8]

Jean Monnet's occasional visits to President Auriol also reflected a great pessimism, as seen through Auriol's journal.

There was a marked contrast between France's impulse to restore itself as a great power, as evidenced in the drive of some of its military leaders, such as General de Lattre, and the utter inability of the country to project in its civilian leadership an image of decisiveness and force. This remained the case for the entire period from General de Gaulle's resignation in January 1946 until the advent of Pierre Mendès France in June 1954. Mendès provided only a short interlude that lasted until February 1955, when the Fourth Republic lapsed again into a cacophony of what Charles de Gaulle called "the voices of division, that is to say, of decadence."[9]

The governments of the Fourth Republic were at the mercy of the National Assembly, which could turn them out by a vote of no confidence at any time. By contrast, the National Assembly could not be dissolved between general elections, which took place every five years (although once during the Fourth Republic, the then Prime Minister, Edgar Faure, took a controversial decision, allowed in the Constitution, to dismiss the Assembly and call for new elections, because two no-confidence votes by absolute majority had taken place within a space of eighteen months).

Even if the chief of state had real powers, which was not the case, the personality of the incumbent Vincent Auriol, while inspiring respect, could in no way inspire awe. Auriol's journal is depressing in its Pollyannaism tinged with pacifism regarding East-West relations and its inflexible and unrealistic attitude toward Germany. To Jean Monnet, in January 1951, Auriol said, "You don't want Germany to be armed, you don't want a German army [but] you accept that there be German unit[s]. Why would you be opposed to a demilitarized and neutralized Germany?"[10]

Auriol and other figures of the Fourth Republic, who participated whether fatalistically or willingly in the farce of French parliamentary democracy, seemed unaware or indifferent to the image that the French government presented to its Western allies and to the world at large: a president without power and a prime minister whose tenure was threatened on a daily basis by the French parliament. It was a ludicrous scene of musical chairs, with prime ministers changing with bewildering rapidity and then reappearing as defense ministers, foreign ministers, or education ministers in succeeding governments. One might ask why this instability, which had prevailed during the interwar period, was allowed to persist after World War II. The new postwar constitution, adopted in October 1946, represented, according to François Mitterrand, "the officialization of anarchy."[11]

Even Auriol, on the most egregious occasions, when delays of weeks occurred in attempts to form a workable government, voiced his frustration: "The international situation . . . is such that I am not amused by these games, which dishonor France in the eyes of the world and discredit the parliamentary and republican regime."[12]

How could anyone associated with this system of government project an image of leadership? As General de Gaulle said, the master theme of the French parliamentary system was that "no head should show above the trenches of democracy."[13] During the tenure of the Fourth Republic (1947–1958), only one of its prime ministers stood out above "the trenches of democracy." Only one prime minister showed the promise of getting something done in his own right: Pierre Mendès France, briefly prime minister from June 1954 until February 1955.

Because Charles de Gaulle had the temerity to question such a system of government laid him open to charges, which struck a chord in the deep-rooted antifascism of the time, that he was a would-be fascist dictator. Vincent Auriol's journal is full of admonitions about de Gaulle, as in this

entry of August 23, 1950: "One can see that [de Gaulle] does not want
organized parties but only one, his own, a single party. This is always the
pattern: the single party leads to personal power, and the latter leads to
dictatorship."[14]

To this view of de Gaulle as a fascist was added the specifically French
notion that the general was a Bonapartist-in-waiting, who would seize
power when the opportunity presented itself and then sanction his rule by
plebiscite. To the Communists, de Gaulle became known as "General Se-
ditious." That de Gaulle in turn branded the Communists as "separatists"
only increased his own isolation in the prevailing antifascist atmosphere
of the period.

Given this continuing instability and wrangling, the United States came
increasingly to the view that France could not be considered a wholly
reliable ally. In addition to its political volatility and its intransigeant stand
against Germany, France's military status in Europe was being undermined gradually by its increasing troop commitment to the colonial war
in Indochina. As of August 7, 1950, according to an announcement of the
defense minister before the National Assembly, the French Armed Forces
totaled 659,000, of whom 150,000 were in Indochina.[15] Put more starkly,
the French had three divisions in West Germany, six in France, and ten
in Indochina in 1950.[16]

Eisenhower favored a grant of independence by France to Indochina,
in which case the French divisions could be brought home to help defend
Europe. Eisenhower could not convince any French leader of the wisdom
of this course, which made the alternative of a German army even more
imperative. But the French were adamantly opposed to this alternative as
well.[17]

Great Britain did not offer any kind of satisfactory alternative. Washington had become more and more aware of the postwar weakness of
Great Britain and more and more disappointed with the lack of a British
commitment toward Europe. It was, therefore, up to the United States to
take the strategic lead in Europe. The idea that French forces would constitute the bulk of the ground troops for the defense of Europe was becoming increasingly unrealistic. Ideally, their numbers should be matched
by German troops. From 1950 onward, the United States, spurred on by
the American military establishment, insistently urged German rearmament on its European partners.

Hand in hand with this sobering American view of Europe's capabilities
emerged a growing hegemonic impulse on the part of the United States.
This was reflected not in the conception of the North Atlantic Treaty, but
in the subsequent creation of the structures of the pact, which culminated
in the naming of the SACEUR in December 1950.

The centralization of authority around the SACEUR and the exclusion
of France from leadership in the flanking maritime commands in the At-

lantic and the Mediterranean had the effect of creating a certain malaise in France, which appears to have been largely unanticipated on both sides of the Atlantic. Unaffected by this malaise was a minority "European current" in the French political class, headed by the centrist René Pleven, who had succeeded Paul Ramadier as minister of National Defense and then had become prime minister in July 1950.

It was this group of "Europeans" who exulted in the fact that France had finally obtained what Aristide Briand, French foreign minister in the 1920s, had vainly sought: an American commitment, in peacetime, to the defense of Western Europe. On March 2, 1950, Pleven said the following before the Committees of National Defense and Foreign Affairs of the National Assembly: "That which Briand could not obtain, the United States in 1950 understood and accepted."[18] However, this "European current" was very much in the minority in French politics.

CONVERSION OF U.S. TO EUROPEAN ARMY IDEA

Because of the uncertainty about the implementation of German rearmament, it still was not clear at the time of Eisenhower's arrival in Europe what forces he would command: whether the separate and distinct forces of the NATO nations or a European Army melded together by a supranational authority known as the European Defense Community. Eisenhower was aware of European sensibilities about German rearmament, and he had to tread carefully: "The more people on my side, the happier I will be," was all Eisenhower would say to a reporter on the question of German rearmament, during a visit to the Rhein Main airbase in January 1951.[19]

Given the continued French intransigeance on German rearmament, the United States had to seriously consider the European Army alternative. In a meeting between President Truman and Prime Minister René Pleven in Washington on January 30, 1951, the president encouraged the French prime minister to pursue the idea of a European Defense Force. A joint communiqué later the same day stated in part, "The Prime Minister . . . referred to the conference to be convened in Paris on February 6th, to consider the formation of a European Army based on European political institutions, and within the framework of the North Atlantic Treaty Organization. The President welcomed the conference and expressed his hope for its success."[20]

It was the first outright statement of U.S. support for the European Army idea and was intended to encourage the work of the participants in the Paris conference—the representative of the six powers of the Coal and Steel Community. According to the NAC decisions at the Brussels meeting the previous December,[21] these delegates were to discuss the application of the Coal and Steel Community idea to that of a European Army.

As we have seen earlier, however, the European Army idea was more of an expedient than a faithful replica of the Coal and Steel Community. As Raymond Aron observed, the European Army was

[an] attempt to apply the method of the Schuman Plan to the solution of the problem created by the American request that Germany be rearmed. The "European" idea was popular; it would carry along the rearmament of Germany, [which was] obviously unpopular. But it was also evident that this conjunction involved the risk of a repercussion in reverse: the unpopularity of German rearmament could carry over to the European idea.[22]

During the summer of 1951, Eisenhower became a convert to the idea of a European Defense Community, largely on the assurances of Jean Monnet.[23] Although at the outset he had been skeptical, he became persuaded that only such a spectacular initiative as the supranational project being proposed could give the necessary fillip to Europe's defense. Eisenhower wrote to Defense Secretary George Marshall on August 3, 1951: "the plan represents the only hope in the immediate future for developing German power—which is of vital importance to us—in conditions acceptable to the other European countries. . . . There will not be real progress toward European unification except through specific projects of this type."[24]

On the day before this memorandum was written, President Truman had approved a joint position of the secretaries of state and defense that the European Army project should go forward, that it should be linked to NATO and the SACEUR, and that Germany should be brought into NATO.[25]

In spite of this convergence of views on the American side, it took more than a year for the decision made by the Brussels North Atlantic Council in December 1950 to result in a clear agreement on German rearmament. In the spring of 1951, a new four-power conference on Germany, the only one to take place in the 1950–1952 period, revealed the French temptations in favor of German demilitarization. The conference ended without results on June 21, 1951, on U.S. initiative. In the same month, the main holders of the "European" idea, the Socialists on the one hand and the Christian Democrats of the *Mouvement Républicain Populaire* on the other, had endured significant losses in elections to the French National Assembly.

It was not until July 24, 1951, that the Paris Conference of the Six produced an interim report. It called for the establishment of a European Defense Community encased in a framework parallel to the Schuman Plan—with a Commissariat, a Council of Ministers, a Parliamentary Assembly, and a Court of Justice. The European force would comprise twenty divisions and 1,800 front-line aircraft by the beginning of 1953.[26] However, Germans and French negotiators were still at odds, chiefly over the size of German units to be admitted to the European Army—The Germans wanted divisions, but the French wanted regimental combat teams.

American frustration mounted at the continuing delays in German rearmament, with the French holding out for a final agreement on the European Army before beginning the recruitment and training of German soldiers. It took another three meetings of the NAC—at Ottawa (September 1951), at Rome (December 1951), and at Lisbon (February 1952)— before the European Army concept (and thus German rearmament) was agreed upon. By the time of the Ottawa meeting, in the words of Dean Acheson,

The bloom was off NATO, the fears of a year before had faded as music wafted westward from the World Festival of Youth and Students for Peace in East Berlin. All this led politicians and writers in Western Europe to question the dangers from the East and the need for rearmament upon which the Americans so continually harped.[27]

The East Berlin meeting referred to by Acheson was followed by a meeting of the World Peace Council in Vienna, called by the Kremlin to coincide with the UN General Assembly session in the fall of 1951.[28] The extraordinary success of the Soviet-sponsored peace movement—culminating in the violent May 1952 demonstrations in Paris against the arrival of Gen. Matthew Ridgway, who replaced General Eisenhower—was a phenomenon hard to comprehend for most Americans, who saw the movement for what it was: a mask to hide the Soviet thrust for world domination. What the Americans failed to perceive was that they were a target of this movement because of their use of the atomic bomb in warfare. Be that as it may, the extraordinary hold of antifascism in the postwar European consciousness, and its amalgamation with the idea of peace—an amalgamation so assiduously cultivated by the Soviets—is evident even in this statement of François Mitterrand in December 1989 (to be sure, before an East German audience): "What you call antifascism is also a certain form of [a] defense of peace and the rejection of an ideology imposed by force."[29]

THE ASCENDANCY OF EISENHOWER AS SACEUR

As we have seen in the previous chapter, Western leaders, led by the Americans, turned to the idea of a supreme commander to shore up a Europe paralyzed by hesitancies (mostly French) over German rearmament. The SACEUR, embodied in the person of Dwight D. Eisenhower, was clearly an afterthought to the creation of NATO. The position had not figured in the NATO structures formed at the first meeting of the

NAC on September 17, 1949. At that time, at least theoretically, the chain of authority went from the NAC to the Defense Committee (made up of defense ministers), and then to the Military Committee (made up of senior military chiefs). The policies that the Military Committee formulated were to be executed by the Standing Group.[30] In addition to the Standing Group in Washington, there were five "regional planning groups" in the field—Northern Europe, Western Europe, Southern Europe, the Western Hemisphere, and the North Atlantic.

The position of SACEUR was suggested later, in the course of the year 1950, as a consensus jelled around the idea of having a unified command for NATO. As noted in Eisenhower's papers, "Eisenhower's new international command would be fitted into a complicated organizational structure."[31] In a sense, the insertion of SACEUR represented a hybridization of Plans B and C discussed between Allied military planners in the period leading up to the first NAC meeting in September 1949.[32] In that earlier period, French officers had complained that Plan C (which had been suggested by the British) was too much like a wartime command.[33] This is, in effect, what was to develop: the spur of the Korean War would militarize the Atlantic alliance.

The place in the hierarchy where SACEUR was positioned was under the direction of the Standing Group.[34] But Eisenhower had been given an important derogation in this regard. In the letter of appointment, which he sent to Marshal Montgomery on March 12, 1951, naming him deputy SACEUR (that is, his personal deputy, with no direct command of troops),[35] Eisenhower stated, "I suggest that you acquaint yourself with the terms of the directive issued to me by the Standing Group, particularly those provisions that authorize direct communications between this headquarters and the several governments of NATO."[36]

Though this Standing Group directive could not be found by the compilers of the Eisenhower Papers (from which this quotation is taken), they cite a NATO Military Committee paper authorizing the Supreme Commander "to communicate with National Chiefs of Staff, and with their respective Defense Ministers, and the heads of government, directly as necessary to facilitate the accomplishment of his mission."[37]

The reality behind this was that Eisenhower, inserted as Supreme Commander and sitting in Europe, was more or less cut loose from the control of the NATO military organ in Washington, the Standing Group.

At the December 1950 NAC meeting in Brussels, most of the Regional Planning Groups were dissolved. By early 1951, Eisenhower had created in their place three regional commands for continental Europe—Northern (at Oslo), Central (at Fontainebleau), and Southern (at Naples). The Standing Group announced its approval of the reorganization on March 20.[38]

Initially, Eisenhower kept the Central Command for himself but managed to convince General Juin to be in charge of land forces under him in this zone.[39] Air forces in the central command were kept separate from the land forces, despite Juin's reservations, and these were placed under the command of Gen. Lauris Norstad.[40]

Thus, Eisenhower, consummate bureaucratic infighter that he was beneath his consensual exterior, had carved out an unassailable position for himself as the military commander of continental Europe. He had direct command over the vital central sector and also authority over the northern and southern sectors. His lack of direct control over the peripheral Atlantic and Mediterranean areas did not matter in terms of his authority over the continent of Western Europe. But even at that, Eisenhower was not happy with the arrangement. As Under Secretary of State Robert Lovett reported to Dean Acheson on December 15, 1950,

General Eisenhower was very unhappy at what he assumed was an effort on the part of the British and our Navy to remove the Mediterranean forces and the North Sea forces from the command of the Supreme Commander. The problem was removed from his mind, however, by the statement of the Joint Chiefs that they would recommend that every American soldier and sailor in that area be placed under him in case of need.[41]

The derogation Eisenhower had received from the Standing Group, under whose control he was theoretically operating, allowed him to have direct contacts with political and defense authorities in the NATO governments. Besides, the Standing Group was far away in Washington, and in any event, Eisenhower continued to communicate directly with Defense Secretary Marshall and the Joint Chiefs of Staff.[42]

In February 1951, an attempt was made by the State and Defense Departments to move the Standing Group and the Committee of Deputies of the NAC to Paris. It was deflected by the Joint Chiefs of Staff on the grounds that it would "subject SACEUR to direct political pressure which might be detrimental to him militarily."[43] In addition, relocating the Committee of Deputies, which was the interim political authority of the alliance, from London to Paris would lessen the military authority of the Standing Group, in which American authority was "more predominant."[44] Defense Secretary Marshall accepted this argument. So, of course, did Eisenhower.[45]

Thus, the Standing Group, visualized by the French as the reincarnation of the Combined Chiefs of Staff in a NATO environment, turned out to be a pale shadow of that wartime body. The SACEUR came to represent the focus of a new American hegemony among the Western powers, not only in terms of U.S. conventional military strength but also in terms of what was seen as the necessity of a sole commander for the nuclear defense of the West.

Outside the control of the SACEUR was the peripheral area of the
Atlantic. The British gave in only with great reluctance to an American
commander in the Atlantic (SACLANT, appointed in January 1952) and
were partly compensated by the creation of a special Channel Command,
which was put in their hands. In addition, the British were given a Mediterranean command based in Malta, which Lord Louis Mountbatten assumed in 1953. However, unlike the SACLANT or even the Channel
Commander, he had to report to the SACEUR rather than directly to the
Standing Group in Washington.[46]

The French were left without a major maritime role. They had sought
a separate French naval commander for the region bordered by Southern
France, Sardinia, and North Africa, because of the need to strengthen the
link between Algeria and the French Metropole. The American position
was that this was not possible without such a French officer being under
the command of CINCSOUTH at Naples, the southernmost of the three
commands under the SACEUR. Here the French ran up against a firm
stand by the Anglo-Americans that control of the seas was primarily their
affair. A Joint Chiefs of Staff position paper on the subject stated that

any change to the Strategic Defense Concept [of NATO] which would impair the
recognition and responsibility of the U.S. and the U.K. for organization and control of the sea lanes or constitute a basis for the designation of a French commander in any theater command arrangements which might develop within NATO
would . . . be unacceptable.[47]

The reorganization of the NATO commands had the effect of effacing
the Western Union's military structure without, however, the abrogation
of the Brussels Pact. The Western Union Chiefs of Staff Committee
(WUCOS) at Fontainebleau gave way to NATO's Central European
Command. In October 1950, internal U.S. proposals approved by Secretaries Acheson and Marshall had called for outright abolition of the Western Union organization.[48] A report of the NATO Military Committee to
the NATO Defense Committee, dated December 12, 1950, put it more
tentatively:

With the establishment of a NATO Command Organization in Europe and the
dissolution of the existing Regional Command Groups . . . it is suggested that the
Brussels Treaty Powers should consider whether it is necessary for them to retain
their own defense organization. It is apparent that when the NATO command
organization is established it will be unnecessary and undesirable to have a parallel
Western Union Command.

If the Brussels Treaty Powers agree that the Western Union Defense Organization should cease to exist as such, this will not prevent Chiefs of Staff or Defense
Ministers [of the Brussels Pact] from meeting. . . . It is considered, however, that
the new headquarters suggested for Western Europe should be directly under

SHAPE and should not be responsible to the Western Union Defense Committee.[49]

The Brussels Pact powers had early on taken the position not to dissolve their pact. A Joint Chiefs of Staff document mentioned the receipt of "a report of a 7 October [1949] meeting of the Western Union Defense Committee in which was discussed the relation between the Brussels Treaty and the North Atlantic Treaty. They agreed that the former Treaty would continue in existence."[50]

It took the intervention of a new NATO body, created at the Ottawa meeting of the NAC in September 1951 to end the impasse over German rearmament and pave the way for the profound reorganization of NATO, which took place at the February 1952 NAC meeting in Lisbon. This body, the Temporary Council Committee, was charged with conducting hearings and forming recommendations on force levels, financing and production, and organizational reform.[51] It was given added weight by the naming of three so-called wise men to its Executive Board: Averill Harriman, Jean Monnet, and Sir Edwin Plowden.[52] The Temporary Council Committee's recommendations were placed before the Lisbon meeting, which came to be known as the Lisbon Force Goals Conference and which represented the culmination of the first phase in NATO's development as a credible defense organization.

By the end of 1951, NATO's military strength had increased to thirty-five active and ready reserve divisions, up from fifteen as of April 1950. By contrast, the Red Army had 103 divisions in Eastern Europe and the western Soviet Union. However, the Western allies did not contemplate a successful defense against the Soviets until mid-1954 and completion of what was called the Medium Term Defense Plan (MTDP).[53] Nevertheless, the admission of Greece and Turkey to NATO, approved at the Lisbon meeting, added another 25 divisions to NATO's forces.[54]

At the Lisbon Force Goals Conference, the number of divisions for the defense of Western Europe was set, albeit at an unrealistically high level (ninety-six divisions by 1954). Also accepted was the creation of the position of Secretary-General of NATO and the formation of a North Atlantic Council in continuous session through the appointment of permanent representatives who would take the place of the Committee of Deputies of the council.

The Lisbon meeting took a favorable position on the European Army plan (which the previous December 1951 NAC meeting in Rome had failed to do), and this led in May 1952 to the signing of the Treaty of Paris, instituting the European Defense Community, subject to ratification by the member countries.

With the Lisbon Conference behind him, and his annual report to NATO an optimistic one, General Eisenhower left Paris on June 1, 1952, after resigning his SACEUR job to return to the United States and run for president. He was succeeded by Gen. Matthew B. Ridgway. All NATO bodies were concentrated in Paris, with the exception of the Standing Group, which remained in Washington.

Although the NATO doctrine would change in the ensuing years, as the character of the Soviet threat changed, the structures of the so-called integrated command had been put in place at Lisbon and would remain so for the next forty-odd years. As Lawrence Kaplan put it, "All things considered, the face of NATO from 1950 to 1952 was drastically altered, producing a visage that essentially would be unchanged to the present."[55]

But the issue of German rearmament was not fully resolved, and it would take another three years, with the death of the European Defense Community and the rise of a straightforward solution—German entry into NATO and the Brussels Pact—for it to be so. German soldiers did not come into the strategic equation until 1955, and during this period, American officials still considered that France was an unreliable and weak partner. It was only after the return of General de Gaulle to power and the decade of the 1960s that Washington officials developed the perception that France could be an unreliable and strong partner.

NOTES

1. National Archives II (NA II), Walter Poole, *The History of the Joint Chiefs of Staff: The Joint Chiefs of Staff and National Policy*, vol. 4, 1950–1952, 198.

2. Ibid.

3. Ibid., 206–07. See also p. 96, Chapter 6.

4. Stephen E. Ambrose, *Eisenhower: Soldier and President* (New York: Simon and Schuster, 1990), 250.

5. Ibid.

6. Georgette Elgey, *La République des illusions* (Paris: Fayard, 1965), 1:465.

7. Charles de Gaulle, *Lettres, Notes et Carnets*, vol. 6 (Paris, Plon, 1984), 111. (Letter to Joseph Paul-Boncour, a prominent senator who had voted against giving powers to Philippe Pétain in July 1940.)

8. Elgey, *La République des illusions*, 215. The two visitors were Maurice Schumann and Pierre-Henri Teitgen.

9. Charles de Gaulle, *Discours et Messages*, vol. II, 1946–1958, *Dans l'attente, Février 1946–Avril 1958* (DM) (Paris: Omnibus/Plon, 1993), 329.

10. Vincent Auriol, *Journal du septennat*, vol. 5, 1951 (Paris: Armand Colin, 1970), 19. (Entry of January 11, 1951.)

11. François Mitterrand, *Mémoires Interrompus* (Paris: Odile Jacob, 1996), 177.

12. Vincent Auriol, *Mon septennat 1947–1954*, ed. Pierre Nora and Jacques Ozouf (Paris: Gallimard, 1970), 357.

13. Charles de Gaulle, *The Complete War Memoirs of Charles de Gaulle*, vol. III, *Salvation, 1944–1946*, trans. Richard Howard (New York: Simon and Schuster, 1964), 962.

14. Auriol, *Mon septennat*, 286.

15. *Informations Militaires* no. 160 (1950): 4.

16. Ambrose, *Eisenhower*, 256.

17. Ibid, 256.

18. *Nouvelles de l'Armée* (February 15–28, 1950): 4.

19. Ambrose, *Eisenhower*, 254.

20. *Harry S. Truman Presidential Library* (HSTL), President's Secretary's Files, Box 186, Communiqué, January 30, 1951.

21. See p. 99, Chapter 6.

22. Raymond Aron and Daniel Lerner eds., *La Querelle de la C.E.D.* (Paris: Armand Colin, 1956), 3.

23. Robert McGeehan, *The German Rearmament Question* (Urbana: University of Illinois Press, 1971), 129.

24. Alfred D. Chandler Jr., ed., *The Papers of Dwight D. Eisenhower*, vol. XII, *NATO and the Campaign of 1952* (Baltimore, Md.: Johns Hopkins University Press, 1989), 459.

25. NA II, Poole, *History of the JCS*, 4: 263.

26. Ibid., 261.

27. Dean Acheson, *Present at the Creation* (New York: W. W. Norton, 1969), 569–70.

28. Ibid., 576.

29. François Mitterrand, *De l'Allemagne, de la France* (Paris: Odile Jacob, 1996), 209.

30. Chandler, *Eisenhower Papers*, 12: 7, n. 2.

31. Ibid.

32. See p. 77, Chapter 5.

33. Ibid.

34. Chandler, *Eisenhower Papers*, 12: 7, n. 2.

35. Ibid., 118.

36. Ibid., 115.

37. Ibid., n. 3. The citation is an excerpt from the report by the North Atlantic Military Committee to the North Atlantic Defense Committee, dated December 12, 1950 (*Foreign Relations of the United States* [FRUS] [1950], vol. 3, Western Europe (Washington, D.C.: Government Printing Office, 1977), 359. The report was adopted by the North Atlantic Council on December 18, 1950.

38. NA II, Poole, *History of the JCS*, 4: 225.

39. *Eisenhower Papers*, 12: 120.

40. Ibid., 122, n. 17.

41. FRUS (1950), 3: 578.

42. NA II, Poole, *History of the JCS*, 4: 225.

43. Ibid., 226.

44. Ibid., 226–27.

45. Ibid., 227.

46. Lawrence S. Kaplan, *NATO and the United States: The Enduring Alliance* (Boston: Twayne Publishers, 1988), 49.

47. NAII, Records Group 218, 1948–59 Geographic Files, Box 97, Section 44, JCS Document 81212 (in reference to a request by the French representative on the Standing Group for a modification of the Defense Plan with regard to the lines of communication linking France with North Africa).

48. NA II, Poole, *History of the JCS*, 4: 207.

49. FRUS (1950), 3: 560.

50. NAII, Records Group 218, 1948–50 Geographic Files, Box 97, 092 Western Europe (3–12–48), Section 36, November 28, 1949, Brief of Metric Papers, November 25, 1949.

51. NA II, Poole, *History of the JCS*, 4: 276.

52. Ibid., 275.

53. Ibid., 226.

54. Kaplan, *NATO and the United States*, 50.

55. Ibid., 51.

PART TWO

EPILOGUE

CHAPTER 8

France and NATO Today: The Attempt at Deconstruction of the SACEUR System

We are going to talk about NATO.

Nothing says that a law cannot have amendments, when it is no longer in accord with custom. Nothing says that a treaty has to be valid in its entirety when its aim has been modified. And nothing says that an alliance has to remain as such when the conditions which were those before it was concluded have [since] changed.

In sum, it is a question of reestablishing a normal situation of sovereignty, in which what is French, in terms of land, sea, air and forces, will only be subject to French authorities. What this means is that it is not a rupture but a necessary adaptation.

Charles de Gaulle, February 21, 1966

Before you, I reaffirm the position of France: the political commitment of the United States in Europe and its military presence on European soil remain an essential factor in the stability and security of the Continent—and also of the world. France is ready to assume its full share in this renovation process. She demonstrated this in announcing a few weeks ago her rapprochment with the military structures of the organization. And I wish to confirm today the spirit of openmindedness and availability with which France approaches this adaptation of NATO, including the military side, as long as the European identity can assert itself fully therein.

Jacques Chirac, February 1, 1996[1]

THE ALLIANCE'S DILEMMAS

The demise of the European Defense Community (EDC) in August 1954 paradoxically paved the way for the almost immediate absorption of

West Germany into the Atlantic Alliance and the creation of a West German Army within NATO. The paradox only proved how misbegotten the EDC idea had been in the first place. But it was the passage of time that had proven the EDC's real enemy. The lessening of the Soviet threat, especially after the death of Stalin in March 1953, made the sacrifice of sovereignty required in the EDC project less and less palatable to the French.

The passage of time also made the prospect of German soldiers bearing arms less difficult for the West Europeans to swallow. By late 1954, the governments of these countries had had five years of experience in dealing with the West German state under its chancellor, Konrad Adenauer.

It was French reticence about ratifying a plan conceived by a Frenchman, Jean Monnet, that had brought about the death of the EDC. This occurred when, on a procedural motion, it was voted down on August 30, 1954, in the French National Assembly. Attributed to French fears of a loss of sovereignty and French concern about a rearmed Germany, the vote had the opposite effect of speeding Germany's rearmament and Germany's rehabilitation (entry into NATO and entry into the Western Union, renamed the Western European Union [WEU]). This transformation was accomplished by the Treaties of London and Paris (October 3 and 23, 1954), less than two months following the rejection of the EDC project by the French National Assembly. A new draft law, which involved no surrender of national defense authority to a supranational body, as the EDC would have done, was finally ratified by the National Assembly on December 30, 1954. After ratification by the Upper House, the Council of the Republic, the EDC Treaty went into effect in May 1955, at which time German rearmament could begin.

But the demise of the EDC also smothered the idea of a European defense identity for the next forty years. As Marie-Pierre Subtil noted, "A number of [French] parliamentarians affirmed [after the vote of the National Assembly on December 30, 1954] that if they had known, they would have chosen the EDC, and thus Europe. Too late."[2]

Although Subtil's statement is technically correct, in that the chance for a European Army was lost, much had already been altered from the original concept, which was supposed to make the EDC a counterpart of the Coal and Steel Community. According to the Treaty of the European Defense Community, signed in Paris in May 1952, this European Army would have had all the trappings of the Coal and Steel Community—a supreme authority, an assembly, and even a court—but the army would have been placed under the command of SACEUR. Thus, the EDC would have been in no way an independent European entity; it would have been under the tutelage, and the command, of the powerful American ally.

With the European Army now out of the question, and thus no possibility of its "cutting across the lines of NATO,"[3] the latter had untram-

meled authority as *the* instrument for collective security in Western
Europe. As *Le Monde* of the period observed, the new accords that arose
as a substitute for the EDC signified "the reinforcement of the structure
of NATO and of the authority of the Supreme [Allied] Commander Europe (SACEUR)."[4]

The upshot was that after a half-dozen years of being forced to choose
among a series of solutions, none of which were wholly satisfactory, the
French had wound up with very little:

- They had no major command other than that of the land forces of the central
  zone.[5]
- They were inside an integrated military structure wholly subordinated to the
  American SACEUR.
- They belonged to a Standing Group, the supposed supreme executive body of
  the military structure, but it was hardly more than a rubber-stamp.
- They were faced with a Britisher—Lord Ismay—as Secretary General of NATO.

Although at the outset, the French welcomed the American-led integrated command as a way of escaping British tutelage, they soon became
uncomfortable with the idea. Already, in July 1951, General Juin described
the central sector command he was about to take over as "too subjugated
to SHAPE."[6] In essence, the French seemed to regard the integrated military command as a sort of zero-sum game that took away their sovereignty: It placed a sizeable proportion of their defense forces under an
American officer. (It is not surprising, given this background, that forty
years later, when the time became ripe for a rapprochement by France
with the military structure of NATO the *sine qua non* of French demands
was that there be created a *permanent*, purely European organ of defense
within the NATO organization.)

THE ALLIANCE'S STRATEGIES

Even with the addition of German troops alongside other Allied forces
in the West, starting in 1955, it was evident, with the explosion of the
Soviet hydrogen bomb in August 1953 and the increase in Soviet conventional forces on the other side of the line in Europe, that the Allied conventional strength was not a match for the Soviets. The Lisbon Force
Goals Conference, with its target of ninety-six NATO divisions by 1954,[7]
had proven to be highly unrealistic economically. Even as the British government was subscribing to the Lisbon Force Goals, it was in the process
of cutting its budget.

As a result, until the late 1950s, the United States was impelled to rely
on its superiority in the number of deliverable nuclear weapons. Conse-

quently, there arose the imperative of brandishing the U.S. nuclear arsenal as an instrument of fear.

Early on General Marshall had presented this notion to Robert Schuman in a Paris meeting on October 4, 1948.[8] At that time, Marshall set forth his philosophy on the relationship between "fear" on the one hand and the atomic bomb on the other. Marshall said the following:

Speaking always completely frankly, as I see the current situation, I think that our best defense lies in the obvious fear that the Russians have of our atomic bomb. From this stems my great preoccupation not to weaken our position in this regard. I know that for a long time the Soviets believed that the atomic weapon was too terrible for us ever to dare use it. Now they know that we will not hesitate to make use of it.[9]

Marshall added that this new appreciation by the Soviets was the basis for the recent softening of their position, and he observed that Moscow would be delighted if a debate were to take place in the United States over whether or not to use the atomic bomb—a debate that Marshall was anxious to avoid. "I think it is very important," said Marshall to Schuman, "that the Russians consider us to be implacable."[10] (It is interesting to note in this regard that in 1945 it was Marshall and Secretary of War Henry Stimson who were among the most determined proponents of an atomic attack against Japan, which they considered necessary to create a psychological shock that was likely to bring the war to a swift conclusion.)[11]

In the aftermath of the Lisbon Force Goals Conference, it became apparent, particularly in Britain and France, that there was not enough public support to fund the massive conventional arms build-up called for by the NAC. At this point, the British turned to the "instrument of fear" approach. This took the form of a Global Strategy Paper of the British Chiefs of Staff, largely inspired by Air Marshal Sir John Slessor. The theme of this paper, which Slessor took to Washington for discussions with American military officials, was that the defense of Europe could be accomplished by means of a threat of strategic nuclear attack on the Soviet Union.

With the advent of the Eisenhower administration in 1953, the "instrument of fear" began to manifest itself under the doctrine of "massive retaliation," articulated by Secretary of State John Foster Dulles in January 1954. The United States would compensate for its inferiority in conventional strength by its dominance in nuclear weapons, ensured by its strategic bomber fleet. As William R. Keylor pointed out,

The strategy of "massive retaliation" . . . could remain a credible deterrent to aggression only so long as the Soviet Union lacked the means to retaliate in kind.

... [It] also depended on the ability of the United States to assure its adversary that aggressive activity in certain strategically situated areas of the globe would automatically trigger an American nuclear response.[12]

Massive retaliation was not, however, enough to reassure the Europeans. The ambiguous U.S. response during the Suez crisis, when the Soviet Union threatened implicitly to rain atomic bombs on Paris and London, created a doubt in the minds of Western Europeans about the solidarity of the American commitment toward them.

The Suez crisis signaled the end of great-power status for Britain, which quickly adapted to the new situation by entering into a sort of privileged subordination to the United States. It was, however, quite different with France, which felt the sting of Suez much more strongly because of the largely false notion that the Algerian rebellion was being masterminded from Egypt. Suez was a large factor in the humiliation of the Fourth Republic, which led indirectly to the return of General de Gaulle less than two years later.

It was little wonder that one of Charles de Gaulle's first major acts after his return to power was to pen the "Memorandum on the Directory" in September 1958, suggesting a "tridominium" of the United States, Britain, and France to manage global, including nuclear, strategy.[13] Interestingly, de Gaulle suggested in his memorandum that discussions on this three-power directory idea be initiated at the ambassadorial level and at the level of the Standing Group[14]—an indication of how this group had become eclipsed in the actual decision-making process in NATO.

The Anglo-Americans paid little attention to de Gaulle's memorandum, as well they might: It was only a pressure tactic, as de Gaulle confided later to his information minister, Alain Peyrefitte:

This memorandum was only a process of diplomatic pressure. I was seeking at the time a way of leaving NATO and regaining my freedom, which the Fourth Republic had taken away. So, I asked for the moon. I knew they would not give it to me. The Anglo-Americans would like to use their force as they see fit, and they do not want us involved. What they want is to dominate us.[15]

The deflection (in effect a rejection) of de Gaulle's memorandum by President Eisenhower set in motion a series of moves by de Gaulle to extricate France from the NATO integrated command, beginning with the withdrawal of the French elements of the NATO Mediterranean Command in 1959 and ending with the withdrawal from the overall NATO military structure in March 1966.

Eisenhower's deflection of de Gaulle's memorandum went almost without saying: The NATO integrated military structure was based on the principle of centralization of command, rationalized in the notion that the defense of Europe was "indivisible." Behind this notion lay the experience of the transition period from the Brussels Pact to the North Atlantic Treaty. European fractiousness, which really meant British-French fractiousness, was such that nothing could be accomplished until the United States took the lead. For something as perilous as defense, compounded by the introduction of nuclear weapons, fractiousness could not be permitted; there had to be a centralized command. In practical terms, this meant that the Americans were in charge, since it was an American officer who was the SACEUR—the Supreme Allied Commander Europe.

In the centralized NATO military structure, not only were all conventional forces under the ultimate command of an American officer, but all nuclear forces in Europe were directly controled by American officers. Furthermore, the employment of the American strategic nuclear arsenal, under the so-called Supreme Integrated Operational Plan (SIOP) was an exclusively American preserve and not briefed in its particulars to the Europeans. Recounting a conversation he had with President John F. Kennedy in May 1961, de Gaulle noted that

in answer to the specific questions I put to him, he was unable to tell me at what point and against what targets, far or near, strategic or tactical, inside or outside Russia itself, the missiles would in fact be launched. "I am not surprised," I told him. "General Norstad, the Allied Commander-in-Chief [SACEUR], whom I hold in the highest esteem and who has shown me every confidence, has never been able to enlighten me on these points, which are vital to my country."[16]

With the change of American administrations from Eisenhower to Kennedy, a revised strategic doctrine emerged, aimed at coping with a new situation: the mounting nuclear threat represented by the Soviet Union, coupled with a clear conventional superiority on its part. The new doctrine of the Kennedy administration was called "flexible response." As Henry Kissinger recounted,

Kennedy was appalled by the cataclysmic consequences of the still-dominant military doctrine of massive retaliation. Under the leadership of his brilliant Secretary of Defense, Robert McNamara, he strove to develop a strategy that created military options other than Armageddon and capitulation. The Kennedy Administration increased the emphasis on conventional forces, and sought to find a discriminating use for nuclear weapons.[17]

The new doctrine, however, was even more disturbing to the Europeans than massive retaliation because it meant that Europe was now more likely to become the battlefield in a series of conventional escalations that might or might not lead to a strategic nuclear exchange. This series of escalations could only lead to death and destruction in Europe. Eventually, the Americans adjusted their strategy to reflect a pure deterrence. This was the so-called balance of terror, officially known as the doctrine of "mutually assured destruction" (MAD).

The Cuban missile crisis of October–November 1962, which revealed Soviet strategic weakness, was both reassuring and disturbing to the Europeans: reassuring, in that it was proof that the United States would not back down in a confrontation with the Soviets; disturbing, in that it showed once again that Europe was at the mercy of American strategic decisions. Later in the decade, American actions in Vietnam convinced the Europeans even more that they were at the mercy of an American policy that might by its actions in Southeast Asia trigger a new world war.

REASONS FOR FRENCH WITHDRAWAL FROM NATO

The notion of the "indivisible" defense of Europe, with an American officer (the SACEUR) in command, however efficient, inevitably left the people in those countries closest to the front line, in particular West Germany, with a feeling of helplessness and impotence. The scheme developed to meet this situation, an all-European nuclear force, over which, however, the Americans had the final say, had a double purpose: to give the Europeans, especially the Germans, a feeling of participation in the operation of NATO's nuclear arsenal and to discourage other European "national" nuclear forces from developing. This meant the French, since the British had already produced a nuclear weapon. This scheme, the Multilateral Force (MLF), was discussed for five years (1960–1965) without ever being accepted by all the West European governments concerned. Finally, a much larger problem took precedence: France's withdrawal from the NATO military structure in March 1966.

The caesura in the France-NATO relationship dating from de Gaulle's letter to Lyndon Johnson on March 7, 1966, was based on two convictions as far as France was concerned: the need to escape the constraints of NATO's integrated command, and thereby reassert the full independence of France, and concomitantly, the need to keep France's nuclear weapons completely outside the NATO command. That the nuclear factor was very much a part of the equation is evident from remarks de Gaulle made to Secretary of State Dean Rusk in two meetings on December 14–15, 1964. De Gaulle in effect said he wanted to wait a few years for France's nuclear weapon to become operational and then he would be prepared to discuss organizational changes in the Alliance.[18]

In 1963, de Gaulle had refused heavy American pressure to join in the Nuclear Non-Proliferation Treaty. By early 1966, de Gaulle had won a long rear-guard struggle to prevent the introduction of the MLF in Europe—a project aimed, as previously noted, at preventing France from developing a nuclear weapon. By the late 1960s, France's nuclear weapon would be virtually operational. All these elements put together argued in favor of putting the integrity of France's nuclear deterrent at the top of Paris' agenda.

The United States's alternate solution to the MLF was the creation, in November 1965, of a ten-member "special committee" of defense ministers (which was to become known as the Defense Planning Committee). Under this ten-member committee—which did not include France, Luxembourg, Norway, Portugal, or Iceland (which has no defense minister)— were created three working groups: Communications, Data Exchange, and Nuclear Planning.[19] It was through the latter, officially called the Nuclear Planning Group (which also did not include France), that the Germans were brought directly into the strategic concepts of NATO nuclear planning; thus, one of the purposes of the stillborn MLF was partly fulfilled.

The discredit brought on American policies by the war in Vietnam and the eventual U.S. defeat there, coupled with the determination of the Soviets to build up their conventional and nuclear forces following their diplomatic setback in the Cuban missile crisis, caused the tide to turn in the late 1970s. The astute diplomacy of Richard Nixon and Henry Kissinger, which had set up a triangular relationship between the United States, China, and the Soviet Union, and which had appeased dissensions in Europe by recognizing the strategic value of the British and French national nuclear forces, could not mask the incontrovertible defeat in Vietnam— despite Kissinger's best efforts to put a good face on the settlement of 1973.

It was only with the advent of the Reagan administration, and with the ensuing American arms build-up and the certitude of President Ronald Reagan's rhetoric, that the tide of the Cold War turned definitively against the Soviets.

THE ATTEMPTED REVIVAL OF THE WESTERN EUROPEAN UNION

During the Cold War, the Brussels Pact and its security organization, the Western European Union, had withered in the face of the all-encompassing presence of NATO as the primary such organization for Europe. In one sense, the Brussels Pact had served its essential purpose: As modified in 1954 after the French failure to ratify the EDC, it had enabled West Germany and Italy to become members of the WEU. This in turn gave more congruence to West Germany becoming also a member of NATO.

Though marginalized, the Brussels Pact had nevertheless remained throughout the Cold War as the one European security organization that had escaped integration into an American system. However, although it had remained in being, it was in an emasculated form, as it had no military forces. These were at the disposal of the SACEUR.

In mid-1973, French Foreign Minister Michel Jobert sought to promote the idea of a European defense identity by proposing that the Defense Committee of the WEU be reactivated. It was only in 1987, however, that the first serious attempt was made—largely French inspired—to revive the dormant Brussels Pact and thereby create a separate European defense entity. The initiative to resuscitate the WEU was embodied in the so-called platform declaration of the pact's council at a meeting in The Hague in 1987. The declaration stated in part:

We, the Ministers of Foreign Affairs and Defense of the member states of the Western European Union . . . recall our commitment to construct a European Union. . . . A major instrument in reaching this objective is the Modified Brussels Treaty [of 1954]. This treaty, which instituted obligations of a considerable import with respect to collective defense, constituted one of the first stages in European unity. . . . Thus we aim at developing a European identity in the defense area which will be more coherent and will reflect more effectively the commitments of solidarity which we subscribed to in the Modified Brussels Treaty and the North Atlantic Treaty.[20]

The impulse to create a European defense identity around the Brussels Pact and its all-important automatic response clause,[21] did not, however, spring from nowhere. As Frédéric Bozo, writing in 1991, stated, this identity "has in effect represented for 40 years the constant ambition of the diplomatic and strategic action of France."[22] The forty years dated from the establishment of the integrated command. The term "European defense identity" is in effect a euphemism for achieving some form of independence from the integrated command or, put another way, for deconstructing the SACEUR system.

Beginning in the mid-1980s, under the aegis of the WEU, European ships and those of NATO took part in joint surveillance activities in the Gulf during the Iran-Iraq war. Similar operations took place during the Gulf War and its aftermath and later in the Adriatic in the 1990s during the enforcement of the embargo against belligerents in the former Yugoslavia (operation Sharp Guard, run jointly by the WEU and NATO).

Still, there were no troops to incarnate a "European defense identity." In the late 1980s, France and West Germany, with France in the lead, sought to create ground forces that were purely European. In 1987, a 4,200-man French-German brigade was created, and the following year, it was placed under the aegis of a new organization, the French-German Defense Council. The latter was created within the framework of the Élysée Treaty of 1963 between the two countries. In October 1991, President François Mitterrand and Chancellor Helmut Kohl announced plans for a purely European force known as the Euro-Corps, with the French-German brigade as its nucleus. Since that time, Belgium, Spain, and Luxembourg have joined the Euro-Corps, whose headquarters at Strasbourg was officially activated on November 5, 1993, and whose strength is projected at 50,000. The contribution of the French to this formation has not been affected by the reorganization of the French Army, which included the end of the draft. Announced in the spring of 1996, this reorganization means, however, that the number of other French troops in Germany will be reduced from 20,000 to approximately 3,000.[23]

Part of the Mitterrand-Kohl Euro-Corps initiative was motivated by a sense of competition with NATO, which was in the process of restructuring itself in the aftermath of the Cold War. NATO's main defense force was to be reorganized into multinational divisions, and a special NATO Rapid Reaction Corps (RRC) under a British commander was to be set up. In a sense, the Euro-Corps was a riposte to the NATO RRC.

The Euro-Corps is not at this point, however, a "projectable" force. The airlift capability does not exist for the rapid projection overseas of a large expeditionary force. Nor does the Euro-Corps have the fully developed and independent intelligence, logistics, and communications capabilities of a modern intervention force. It is, however, a force that exists and is capable of being used, provided that the two original sponsors, Germany and France, agree to its use. This depends, particularly in Germany, on political considerations, namely parliamentary approval for the use of German forces externally.

FRANCE'S DIFFICULT ROAD BACK TO NATO

The "NATO miracle" worked wonders for some forty years. What seemed so tentative in 1949, so problematic—a credible defense of Western Europe in the face of a huge Soviet army—had become effortlessly efficient, though unused, by the time the Berlin Wall came down forty years later. At that moment, the NATO instrument—the unified command—became more important than the purpose for which it was created, Though the threat had gone, the instrument remained as a testimony to the unity of Europe—under American aegis.

The instrument had been fashioned to defend against the threat of a massive attack from the east. This required a highly centralized command, both for the use of conventional and nuclear weapons. The imperative of the integrated command was that of maximum efficiency. It was not an instrument to be easily thrown away. Still, the unreconstructed school of thought in France is that the integrated command must go:

Integration *is* the SHAPE and the SACEUR. [SACEUR's] role is predominant, his prerogatives are exhorbitant. . . .
[The SHAPE/SACEUR system] is anachronistic. It is not necessary to defend Europe at present. We have a complately changed universe. . . . There is only one

real reform [of NATO] that has a basis in reality, and that has to do with who commands.[24]

Although the integrated command theoretically was an anomaly with the end of the Cold War, it nevertheless turned out in Bosnia that nothing was possible until the Americans intervened and exercised the facilities of the integrated command. The virtue of the integrated command—American participation and know-how—was once again seen as crucially important, despite its vice—the increasingly anachronistic deficit of sovereignty for the West European countries.

As Diego Ruiz-Palmer pointed out, the relationship between France and NATO after the caesura of 1966 has been based in part "on joint military action, but at the same time . . . , on the mutual recognition of a strategic disagreement in the nuclear area and on the non-participation of an ally in an integrated military structure considered by the other members of NATO as the keystone of [a] common defense."[25]

It is worth noting that, of the many agreements concluded between France and NATO since 1966—beginning with the Lemnitzer-Ailleret Accords of 1967 on operations in the central zone of Europe, through the Lanxade-Naumann-Shalikashvili agreement of 1993 on placing the Euro-Corps under NATO in a time of emergency—none touched on the use of France's nuclear deterrent. According to the chief of staff of the French armed forces, writing in 1981, "The cooperation [between France and NATO] concerns only conventional forces and excludes, therefore, any planning for the utilization of nuclear forces."[26] France's *force de frappe*, consequently, has remained for the last thirty years a factor of uncertainty, in the defense of Western Europe.

With the end of the Cold War, however, nuclear deterrence has taken on a lesser importance, a fact which was acknowledged by French President Jacques Chirac in a speech shortly after the NAC meeting in Berlin in early June 1996: "In the new international context, nuclear deterrence will not occupy the same place as during the Cold War. It was then the keystone arch of our defense, in the sense that our whole military apparatus was subordinated to it."[27]

The French nuclear deterrent, never palpably operational during the Cold War, lives on, but in a reduced status and in the background. In the words of President Chirac, "Deterrence still constitutes the ultimate assurance of our security and the guarantee of our independence."[28] But the French nuclear deterrent also overhangs the European scene as a sort of existential threat: France can obliterate Germany but the reverse is not at present true. However, the threat is not real; this very expensive instrument is not to be used, according to the French president: "The nuclear strategy of France will of course remain [that of] deterrence and therefore defensive, excluding—it goes without saying—all idea of battle."[29]

The French nuclear deterrent is a weapon—or a concept—in search of a mission. This becomes relatively straightforward in the case of Great Britain, France's only other nuclear partner in Western Europe. France and Great Britain have been engaged in regular discussions on nuclear strategy since 1993.[30] French officials, up to and including President Chirac, have described these discussions as fruitful and important, without being much more specific than that. Chirac has said only that the French and British deterrent forces have a role to play in the common security policy of the European Union. At the same time, he has assured audiences that there is no intention to come up with a French or Anglo-French nuclear guarantee as a substitute for the American deterrent in Europe. The intention, rather, is to reinforce deterrence overall.[31]

It is with continental Western Europe that the problem becomes more complicated, and this was evident with the unrest stirred in Germany and elsewhere in the brief period of French resumption of nuclear testing in the Summer of 1995. In September 1995, and obviously partly as a palliative, Prime Minister Alain Juppé raised the notion of "concerted deterrence" between France and its European neighbors—again without further specifics. It is not clear as yet what "concerted deterrence" involves, but President Chirac has made clear what it does not involve: "It is not a question of enlarging our deterrence or of imposing on our partners a new contract. It is [rather] a question of taking into account the consequences of a community of destiny, of an increasing intertwining of our vital interests."[32]

With the French nuclear deterrent now of reduced importance, the French desire to stay apart from NATO as a means of retaining the independence of the *force de frappe* has lost much of its intensity. In the 1960s, however, this was a very real consideration.[33]

The softening of this negative constraint on France being linked to NATO's military organization has been accompanied by new, positive incentives for France to draw closer to NATO. The end of the Cold War has unleashed the West's potential to intervene more freely in areas of crisis. Not only does Russia have a much reduced capacity to oppose such interventions than did the former Soviet Union, it is more disposed to join in such ventures, as was demonstrated in the Intervention Force (IFOR) operation in Bosnia-Herzegovina. This means that intervention capability, rather than nuclear deterrence, has been given pride of place. According to Jacques Chirac, "The strategy of action, which lies with conventional forces that are autonomous and projectable, with reliable command capabilities, and with diversified means of intelligence, has developed a new importance."[34]

This "strategy of action" by "projectable" forces—what could be called Chirac's epiphany of 1996—has impelled France to draw closer to NATO, where the know-how and the capability for external action exists.

In addition to the lessening importance of nuclear weapons and the newly favorable climate for intervention, there is another reason for France's rapprochement with NATO at this time: the diminished American military presence—and therefore influence—in Europe following the end of the Cold War.

An alliance reflects the relative political weight of its members and, as time goes on, changes in these relative weights. During the Cold War, the weight of the United States vis-à-vis its European partners was overwhelming. The survival of Europe and the Western world depended on the efficiency of the U.S. nuclear deterrent force. The defense of Europe, in order to be at a top level of performance, both nuclear and conventional, had to be under American control. The presence of some 350,000 U.S. military personnel in Europe was not only a guarantee of the U.S. commitment to defend the Continent; it was a reinforcement of the American predominance in NATO. The American military presence in Europe is now 100,000, less than a third of what it was at the height of the Cold War. Western Europe does not at present need the U.S. nuclear umbrella, and it no longer needs the United States in order to defend itself.

With the relative political weight of the U.S. within NATO clearly reduced as a result of the end of the Cold War (1989) and the break-up of the Soviet Union (1991), two major developments took place within NATO. First, there was a perceived need to adapt NATO's rigid chain of command, now that the "indivisible" defense of Europe was no longer required. Second, with the relative weight of the United States within NATO reduced, France could not only feel freer to challenge existing NATO doctrines and procedures, it could also move closer to the NATO structures without the fear of loss of sovereignty that existed during the Cold War. Indeed, the ease with which France has been able to effect changes—at least in theory—in the NATO structure is a reflection of these changing political weights. The United States for its part also felt disposed to show greater flexibility and a greater sense of accommodation.

As Diego Ruiz-Palmer noted, one of the paradoxes of the France-NATO relationship following 1966 was that

of an ally who, while accepting the hypothesis of joint military action and the necessity of preparing it and of devoting effective military means to it when the time came, placed itself, by its own volition, outside the political-military and military bodies of the Alliance, in which were decided the strategic principles and the operational modalities which would govern, on the ground, this joint action.[35]

This outsider situation, difficult for France operationally after the caesura of 1966, became more and more onerous as the cold war wore off. As the only major power in Europe, other than Britain, able to join in foreign interventions in the freer atmosphere of the post–Cold War era,

France needed to take steps to overcome the disadvantages of its isolation from the NATO military bodies.

The process was slow and halting under the long presidency of François Mitterrand. Jacques Attali quoted Mitterrand as saying, "During the cohabitation [of 1986–1988] we were within [the snap of a finger] of a return to integration in NATO. It was my refusal which prevented it."[36]

As with the process of German reunification, Mitterrand found himself clinging to archaic nostrums aimed at retaining France's preeminent position on the Continent. He refused to subscribe to the new NATO doctrine advanced at the NAC summit in London in July 1990—the use of nuclear weapons only as a last resort—because it denigrated the value of the French nuclear deterrent. Mitterrand stated the following in a press conference on July 6, 1990:

They announce that nuclear weapons will not be used except after the fact, after a conventional war. . . . This seems to be completely antinomic with French strategy, which is not to take the initiative to resort to force, but which keeps the option to use all of its forces at the desired moment, the latter having as much as possible to precede the opening of the conflict.[37]

Or, as Mitterrand is reported to have stated privately to President George Bush in a letter sent a week earlier: "Deterrence, in order to be effective, must be early. It is both the most effective and the least perilous solution."[38]

Yet, a year and a half later, during which France had participated in the coalition war against Iraq, the French subscribed to and indeed participated in the elaboration of NATO's new strategic concept. Announced at the Rome NAC summit in December 1991, the concept instituted sweeping changes, including operations outside the original zone of the North Atlantic Treaty, new peacetime operations for the alliance, and the use of nuclear weapons only as a last resort. Although the French in press statements made known their reserves on the latter point, they subscribed to the concept. As Ruiz-Palmer noted,

Once France had subscribed in 1991 to the same Strategic Concept of the Alliance as its allies, and once the distinction between integrated forces and nonintegrated forces no longer covered either a political need or a tangible military reality, it became less and less conceivable that France could continue to remain apart from the decision-making bodies of the Alliance.[39]

A still more significant change in the France-NATO relationship took place in January 1993 when France, having been encouraged by Germany, agreed that the Euro-Corps could come under NATO command in a time of military emergency.

By the middle of the 1990s, it was clear that the French had shifted tactics. Rather than try to create a wholly separate defense identity around the WEU, with all that implied in terms of cost and redundancy of effort, they announced their readiness to create a distinctly European defense "pillar" within NATO. In return, they would expect a "reform" of NATO, which would involve, though not stated outright, a deconstruction of the SACEUR system.

For the short term, the French support the creation of distinctly European commands within NATO: the so-called Combined Joint Task Forces (CJTFs). For the longer term, an overall revision of the NATO command structure is anticipated, as evoked in the communiqué of the NAC summit in Berlin on June 3, 1996: "The Military Committee's Long Term Study . . . will result in recommendations for a military command structure better suited to current and future *Euro-Atlantic* security" (emphasis added).[40]

The creation of CJTFs had been agreed to in principle at the Brussels NAC summit in January 1994. However, the United States initially conceived the CJTFs as embedded in the various regional commands under the SACEUR. The issue then entered into a long stalemate.

On December 5, 1995, France made a new gesture. It announced that it was returning to the NATO Military Committee (made up of the chiefs of staffs of the member countries) and would also attend sessions of NATO ministers of defense when those meetings are considered NAC meetings. The return of France to the NATO Military Committee and its associated bodies was a significant symbolic step. However, as previously indicated, there had long since been a series of agreements which, if not linking France to NATO, provided for cooperation between the two parties in various areas and in different sorts of emergencies.

Finally, a political-military framework was endorsed at the Berlin NAC summit in June 1996, centered on the CJTFs as the expression of the European defense and security identity within NATO—under the formula "separable but not separate," which had first been evoked at the January 1994 Brussels summit. The United States conceded the point that the CJTFs can be "national," located outside the integrated command, provided that they can be brought up to the level of NATO standards. Details on how the CJTFs would operate were in theory to be worked out subsequently. In the view of American officials, the CJTFs, or "national nuclei," would be skeletal and would not come up to strength until and unless an operation were envisaged.

Theoretically, under this new dispensation, a CJTF under the auspices of the WEU could manage a remnant NATO force in Bosnia should American ground troops be withdrawn from there. In this way, NATO's logistical and airlift capabilities would be used by the CJTF, and these would likely include some American personnel. But it would be a European operation commanded by Europeans and sponsored and planned by the WEU. Although American military officers find it hard to visualize an intervention operation in which they would not be fully involved, the idea of European-led operations remains an important principle to the French.

In the view of American officials, NATO assets that would be used collectively in a WEU-led operation, such as Airborne Warning and Control Systems (AWACS), airfields, and communications facilities, would be subject to the control of the SACEUR (who is an American), in his capacity as a supporting commander. Though American officials prefer to call this "operational command," the *control* that the SACEUR would exercise seems to be more in the French sense of the word (monitoring) rather than the English sense. The SACEUR, as a supporting commander, would not be in the immediate theater of operations. This was the case during the Gulf War, when American troops from the SACEUR's command fought in the desert under the Central Command (CENTCOM) of Gen. Norman Schwarzkopf.

In practical terms, the control or command exercised by the SACEUR in WEU-led operations would consist, according to American officials, of the right to demand reports from the WEU on the way the NATO assets are being used and the right to remove American personnel from a WEU-led operation should it be deemed necessary. It is hardly likely that the U.S. Congress will not want to have a say in how these arrangements are developed.

In the wake of the agreement in principle reached at the Berlin NAC summit (June 1996), President Chirac announced that France was resuming its full place at meetings of NATO defense ministers whenever they take place. However, France has not yet returned to the integrated military structure of NATO, nor has it joined the Defense Planning Committee and the Nuclear Planning Group—both created around the time of the French departure from the NATO military structure and considered by the French to be part of the integrated command. Nevertheless, though not joining in the sessions of the Nuclear Planning Group, France announced its willingness to discuss nuclear matters with the United States. This was declared by President Chirac during a visit to the United States on February 1, 1996. Presumably, if details are satisfactorily worked out on the CJTFs and other "reform" issues, France would then announce its full return to the NATO military structure.

Another aspect of the NATO "reform" process, and thus of France's full return to NATO, is the redistribution of roles in the revised NATO command structure, which are likely to be reduced to two commands (North and South) under the SACEUR. The French have already made known that they would like to have a European officer placed in charge of the Southern Command in Naples.[41] If this were to happen, which is unlikely given the opposition of the U.S. as the predominant naval power in the Mediterranean, it would be a rectification of the original arrangements in 1951 whereby France was excluded from a major NATO command.[42]

The "reform" of NATO is supposed to be accomplished before the anticipated enlargement of NATO to the east. Indeed, NATO may be so transformed by the reform process that it may be unrecognizable, and it may become a more palatable organization in the eyes of the Russians. In the Berlin NATO communiqué of June 3, 1996, three objectives for NATO were set out:

1. Building a European security and defense identity within NATO.
2. Undertaking new roles and missions relating to conflict prevention and crisis management and proliferation of weapons of mass destruction, while maintaining capability for collective defense.
3. Broadening and deepening dialogue and cooperation with the partners, notably through the Partnership for Peace and the North Atlantic Cooperation Council.[43]

THE WEU AS A DEFENSE INSTRUMENT

As an instrument of defense, the WEU poses a number of problems. According to Christoph Bertram,

The WEU is . . . ill-equipped to meet needs that NATO cannot, such as the practical pooling of European defense resources. This inability is being institutionalized by its peculiar composition, which rolls together four different types of affiliation: *full members*, that is, countries that are members of both NATO and the EU; *observers*, countries that are members of the EU but not of NATO . . . ; *associate members*, European countries that are members of NATO but not of the EU . . . ; and *associate partners*, countries in Eastern Europe (including the three Baltic states) with which the EU has entered into Association Agreements.[44]

Since some members of the WEU do not belong to NATO (e.g., Ireland), and some members of NATO do not belong to the EU (e.g., Turkey, the United States and Canada), the WEU therefore, as a security organization, will most often be used in a mode of "variable geometry," to used a French-inspired phrase: Some members would have to be kept out of the play, especially if NATO assets are to be used. This makes for a great deal of incoherence, in contrast to the way NATO was developed, as an organization with an integrated command directing the "indivisible defense" of Europe. In the WEU, the potential is there for more incoherence rather than less because all countries who join the EU are eligible for membership in the WEU. This opens the prospect of a further diffusion resulting from the entry of neutral countries into the EU, which is now taking place, because they could possibly become members of the WEU in the future.

The linking of the EU/WEU with NATO raises the question of what American officials call the "back door guarantee." To draw an extreme example, would the United States, because of a NATO-WEU link, become committed at some future point to protect the territorial integrity of Sweden? This issue is apart from, but related to, the question of NATO enlargement: If Poland, Hungary, and the Czech Republic were to become full members of NATO by, say, the year 2000, this would mean that the United States and the other countries of NATO would be obliged to come to their defense if they were attacked. In this situation, could the pro-Western neutrals in the EU (e.g., Austria and Finland) remain aloof from NATO while several former Communist countries come inside the NATO tent and receive a security guarantee?

In the midst of all this present (and future) confusion, there seems to be room for an expanded role of the "Quad"—the four countries within NATO that originally met on the margins of NATO meetings to discuss Berlin issues: The United States, the United Kingdom, France, and West Germany. In the 1970s under the encouragement of Henry Kissinger, the group began meeting separately for discussions on a variety of international issues.

The "Quad" as a venue for discussions on strategic issues takes on added congruence in the face of France's rapprochement with NATO. Indeed, most of the crucial issues on NATO "reform" have been discussed within the Quad framework. This "Quad" factor has not gone unnoticed. On June 11, 1996, in the wake of the NATO Berlin Summit, Belgium's foreign minister, Erik Derycke, stated his country's opposition to the creation of a "directory" of several "great powers" who would reserve to themselves the important decisions in matters of European security. *Le Monde* commented that "these words are aimed at the meetings which are held among the United States, Great Britain, Germany, and France for the purpose of preparing decisions within NATO."[45]

In some ways it is more logical and coherent for the main European institution, the European Union, to take over the role of Europe's security and defense, rather than the WEU. In the words of Jacques Chirac,

Our goal must be to make the European Council [of the European Union] the supreme body of orientation and decision in this domain [of our European policy of joint defense], particularly vis-à-vis the WEU. It is thus, and only thus, that we can make a coherent and overall plan based on what we have accomplished so far in our different projects of bilateral cooperation.[46]

The WEU is charged by the Maastricht Treaty with looking into a defense policy for the European Union, in connection with the ongoing Intergovernmental Conference (IGC) of the EU. The existence of the WEU is, however, contingent, since the Brussels Pact is due for renewal in 1998. This fact is also mentioned in the Maastricht Treaty and thus presents the question of whether the WEU would continue its existence after 1998 or be folded into the European Union.

Many Europeans, including and especially the French, seem to prefer that the WEU disappear into the EU when the Brussels Pact term comes up, but those who oppose a defense role for the European Union, that is, Britain, are firmly against a melding of the WEU into the EU. The British, the true soulmates of Charles de Gaulle in the institutional sense, are loath to give any part of their sovereignty in the defense area to a European institution. Since the British are founding members of the Brussels Pact, there seems little prospect that the WEU will disappear into the EU at any time in the near future.

Moreover, there are negative connotations to the EU, which began as an institution of economic cooperation, acquiring the trappings of a defense organization. Moreover, the EU seems a long way from developing the Common Foreign and Security Policy (CFSP) evoked tentatively in the Maastricht Treaty; and without a functioning and credible CFSP, it would be premature for the EU to develop into a defense organization. The lesson of the European Defense Community forty years ago is testimony to the fallacy of this inversion of approach.

REFLECTIONS

Fifty years after the Victory, France found itself in a distinctly altered position from that of the weak France of the postwar period. The France of that earlier period turned in the first instance toward an alliance with its prewar ally, Britain. The hopes of yet another revival of the Entente Cordiale, emerging in early 1948, quickly evaporated. The new partnership of Britain and France rapidly turned into a duel, as Maurice Vaïsse put it.[47]

Even before the ink was dry on the Brussels Pact, its original aim—the addition of the Benelux cluster to the French-British core of the Dunkirk Pact—was being transformed: The French had made their own approach to the United States for a bilateral military relationship; the British were already working toward separate "Anglo-Saxon" talks with Washington; and the transcendance of the forthcoming Brussels Pact by a more credible security organization was already in the air.

As the Brussels Pact approaches the end of its fifty-year lifespan in 1998 and faces either extension or extinction, the unchanging nature of the French-British incompatibility seems clear. There are a few areas where this principle is contradicted, but these remain the exceptions that prove the rule: notably the cooperation between the two countries' air forces and in the French-British nuclear dialogue, which began in 1993.

In conclusion, one can say that during the entire period that led from the Victory to NATO, France was never able to fix its position satisfactorily vis-à-vis Great Britain. It was never able to appear equal with Great Britain in the eyes of the United States. There was a sort of unstated complicity between the British and the Americans aimed at maintaining France at a level below that of Britain. This would have its sequel later on in the 1950s at the time of the debate over the European Defense Community. The EDC would have obliged the French—but not the British—to meld themselves into a European defense ensemble and thereby surrender some elements of their national sovereignty.

Thus, when the occasion arose in the 1960s, during which time General de Gaulle twice vetoed the entry of Great Britain into the Common Market, it was not so much a sign of ingratitude toward his wartime ally (although, as Alfred Grosser observed, "Forgetting offenses is not a Gaullist virtue").[48] Rather, it was to mark before the world the end of this ephemeral disequilibrium that existed between Great Britain and France between 1940 and the 1960s. Also, it was to mark France's desire for hegemony over the continent of Western Europe.

In contrast to the ever-deficient Entente Cordiale, it is the French-German alliance that has become the constant of the European political scene—as though that three-generational period when Germans hated Frenchmen and Frenchmen hated Germans was a thing of the past, and reconciliation had become a permanent necessity. The many links built up since the Élysée Treaty of 1963, especially in the military area with the Euro-Corps, and in the French-German biennial Summit meetings, are vibrant testimonials to this new fact of life in Europe.

CONCLUSION

Throughout the entire period since the creation of the NATO structures, the French have displayed a remarkable continuity of purpose: to prevent the British from being in a position superior to them; and to find a means of controlling Germany, preferably by means of an alliance. The quest for parity (or more) with the British is evident even today, in the French request to be given the CINCSOUTH Command at Naples.

Strategically, French aims during this entire period can be summed up in the concept of a European defense identity which, as we noted earlier, has been described by Frédéric Bozo as a constant of French policy over the past forty years. The concept provides a way of excluding the British except on French terms which the British, always chary about committing themselves militarily on the Continent, would be unlikely to accept. The concept keeps Germany penned in Europe, as a member of a continental strategic alliance with the French.

Finally, a European defense identity, as it has come to be interpreted by Jacques Chirac, consists of both a certain independence of decision and command vis-à-vis the U.S. but also, due to limited French resources, a certain dependence on U.S. logistical and other support.

The key in this still far from secure strategic edifice is the durability of the alliance with Germany. It is of course possible, though there are no serious indications as yet, that the new coalition of France and Germany will fall apart. If this alliance should fail, and France turn once again back to Britain, the result would never be a European federation. Rather it would be something like a return to the 19th Century Concert of European nations.

The French-German Common Security and Defense Concept, which was drawn up in December 1996 and surfaced in the press at the end of January 1997, is a recognition of the high stakes involved in the preservation of this alliance: "The community of destiny which unites France and Germany rests particularly on a consensus concerning fundamental questions of strategy and society. . . . Our security interests are more and more inseparable."[49]

Whatever happens in the coming years, there will be no European federal entity without the Franco-German coalition. As Victor Hugo wrote in the nineteenth century,

[Europe] is composed essentially of France and Germany. The alliance of France and Germany is the constitution of Europe. . . . Civilization is essentially Germany and France. . . . It is necessary, for the universe to be in equilibrium, that there be in Europe, as the double keystone arch of the continent, two great states of the Rhine.[50]

NOTES

1. "France and NATO," *Radio France Inter*, "Le téléphone sonne," February 8, 1996 (Voices of Charles de Gaulle and Jacques Chirac).

2. Marie-Pierre Subtil, "L'échec du projet de défense européenne," *Le Monde*, August 20–21, 1989, 2.

3. See p. 98, Chapter 6.

4. "De la Communauté européenne de défense aux textes signés à Londres par les 'Neuf'," *Le Monde*, October 7, 1954, 2.

5. General Juin assumed command of all forces within this zone in 1953.

6. Vincent Auriol, *Mon septennat 1947–1954* (Paris: Gallimard, 1970), 354. (Letter from Juin to President Auriol, July 10, 1951.)

7. Lawrence S. Kaplan, *NATO and the United States: The Enduring Alliance* (Boston: Twayne Publishers, 1988), 51. See also p. 113, Chapter 7.

8. See p. 59, Chapter 4, for other details on this meeting.

9. *Archives of the Quai d'Orsay* (AQ), Europe 1944–1960, Généralités (Bloc occidental), Dossier 22, Alliance Occidentale: The Brussels Pact and the Defense of Europe, May 1948–June 1949, Interview between Marshall and Schuman, 9:30 a.m., October 4, 1948, 4.

10. Ibid.

11. "Neither Stimson nor General Marshall was concerned over whether the bomb should be used on Japan, only with how to use it to stop the slaughter as soon as possible" (David McCullough, *Truman* (New York: Simon and Schuster, 1992), 393.

12. William R. Keylor, *The Twentieth Century World: An International History* (New York: Oxford University Press, 1996), 285.

13. See p. 80, Chapter 5.

14. See also p. 80, Chapter 5.

15. Alain Peyrefitte, *C'était de Gaulle* (Paris: Fayard, 1994), 352.

16. Charles de Gaulle, *Memoirs of Hope: Renewal and Endeavor* (MH), *Part 1, Renewal 1958–1962*, trans. Terence Kilmartin (New York: Simon and Schuster, 1971), 257–58.

17. Henry A. Kissinger, *Diplomacy* (New York: Simon and Schuster, 1994), 612.

18. Lyndon B. Johnson Presidential Library (LBJL), Multilateral Force Cables, Box 24, vol. 3(1): Paris telegram SECTO 12, December 14, 1964, Section 3, p. 3; and Paris telegram SECTO 26, December 16, 1964, section 2, p. 1.

19. Henry W. Degenhardt, ed., *Treaties and Alliances of the World* (Detroit: Gale Research Company, 1986), 212.

20. Bernardette Armaillé, *L'Architenture européenne de sécurité* (Paris: CREST, 1991), 47.

21. See p. 40, Chapter 3.

22. Frédéric Bozo, *La France et l'OTAN: De la guerre froide au nouvel ordre européen* (Paris: Masson, 1991), 195.

23. *Le Monde*, July 12, 1996, 5.

24. Remarks made by Gabriel Robin, former French ambassador to NATO, on February 10, 1996, at a conference entitled "France and NATO," held under the auspices of the Center for Defense Historical Studies in Paris. (N.B. SHAPE is the acronym for Supreme Headquarters, Allied Powers Europe and is now located in Mons, Belgium).

25. Diego A. Ruiz-Palmer, "La coopération militaire entre la France et ses alliés, 1966–1991: entre le poids de l'héritage et les défis de l'après-guerre froide," in *La France et l'OTAN, 1949–1996*, ed. Maurice Vaïsse, Pierre Mélandri, and Frédéric Bozo (Brussels: Éditions Complexe, 1996), 569.

26. Ibid., 578.

27. *Press Service of the Presidency*, Speech of Jacques Chirac to the Institute of Higher Studies of National Defense (IHEDN), June 8, 1996, 5.

28. Ibid.

29. Ibid., 3.

30. Daniel Vernet, "La révolution stratégique chiraquienne," *Le Monde*, June 8, 1996, 12.

31. President Chirac's speech to IHEDN, 6.

32. Ibid., 6–7.

33. See pp. 125–26, this chapter.

34. President Chirac's speech to IHEDN, 5.

35. Ruiz-Palmer, "La coopération militaire entre la France et ses alliés," 569.

36. Jacques Attali, *Verbatim III, 1988–1991* (Paris: Fayard, 1995), 399. N.D.L.R. "Cohabitation" meant that one party controled the presidency and another the National Assembly and therefore the prime ministership. In that period, Jacques Chirac was prime minister.

37. *Le Monde*, July 8–9, 1990, 5.

38. Attali, *Verbatim III*, 526.

39. Ruiz-Palmer, "La coopération militaire entre la France et ses alliés," 598.

40. *NATO Press and Media Service*, Press Communiqué M-NAC-1 (96) 63, 2.

41. *Le Monde*, July 21–22, 1996, 3. At present there are two other commands under the SACEUR: the Northern, at High Wycombe in the United Kingdom; and the Central, at Brunssum in the Netherlands.

42. See p. 121, this chapter.

43. NATO Press Communiqué M-NAC-1 (96) 63, 2.

44. Christoph Bertram, *Europe in the Balance: Securing the Peace Won in the Cold War* (Washington, D.C.: Carnegie Endowment, 1995), 80.

45. *Le Monde*, June 13, 1996, 2.

46. President Chirac's speech to IHEDN, June 8, 1996, 9. The different projects referred to include the Euro-Corps, the air operations cooperation between France and Great Britain, and the maritime operations cooperation among France, Italy, and Spain.

47. Maurice Vaïsse, "L'Échec d'une Europe franco-britannique ou comment le pacte de Bruxelles fut créé et délaissé," in *Les Débuts de la construction européenne*, Raymond Poidevin, ed. (Brussels: Bruylant, 1986), 369.

48. Alfred Grosser, *Affaires extérieures: la politique de la France, 1944–1984* (Paris: Flammarion, 1989), 158. (This was in reference to de Gaulle's refusal to attend the twentieth anniversary in 1964 of the Normandy landings, from which the general's Free French forces were excluded.)

49. *Le Monde*, January 30, 1997, 12.

50. Claude Julien, "L'outil et le projet," *Le Monde Diplomatique*, April 1996, 16.

Selected Bibliography

BOOKS

Acheson, Dean. *Present at the Creation: My Years in the State Department*. New York: W. W. Norton, 1969.

Ambrose, Stephen E. *Eisenhower: Soldier and President*. New York: Simon and Schuster, 1990.

Aron, Raymond. *La querelle de la C.E.D*. In *Studies by Jacques Fauvet and Others*, edited by Raymond Aron and Daniel Lerner. Paris: Armand Colin, 1956.

Attali, Jacques. *Verbatim III, 1988–1991*. Paris: Fayard, 1995.

Auriol, Vincent. *Journal du septennat, 1947–1954*. Paris: Armand Colin, 1974.

———. *Mon septennat 1947–1954*. Ed. Pierre Nora and Jacques Ozouf. Paris: Gallimard, 1970.

Azéma, Jean-Pierre, and François Bédarida, eds. *La France des années noires*. Vol. I, De la défaite à Vichy. Paris: Seuil, 1993.

Ball, George W. *The Past Has Another Pattern: Memoirs*. New York: W. W. Norton, 1982.

Bertram, Christoph. *Europe in the Balance: Securing the Peace Won in the Cold War*. Washington, D.C.: Carnegie Endowment, 1995.

Bidault, Georges. *D'une résistance à l'autre*. Paris: Les Presses du Siècle, 1965.

Billotte, Pierre. *Le passé au futur*. Paris: Stock, 1979.

———. *Le temps des armes*. Paris: Plon, 1972.

Bischof, Gunter, and Stephen E. Ambrose, eds. *Eisenhower: A Centenary Assessment*. Baton Rouge: Louisiana State University Press, 1995.

Bozo, Frédéric. *La France et l'OTAN: De la guerre froide au nouvel ordre européen*. Paris: Masson, 1991.

Bundy, McGeorge. *Danger and Survival: Choices about the Bomb in the First Fifty Years*. New York: Vintage Books, 1990.

Condit, Doris M. *History of the Office of the Secretary of Defense*. Vol. 2, *The Test of War, 1950–1953*. Washington, D.C.: Historical Office, Office of the Secretary of Defense, 1988.

Condit, Kenneth W. *The History of the Joint Chiefs of Staff: The Joint Chiefs of Staff and National Policy*. Vol. II, 1947–1949. Wilmington, DE: Michael Glazier, 1979.

Debré, Michel, *Trois républiques pour la France: Mémoires* II: *Agir, 1946–1958*. Paris: Albin Michel, 1988.

Doise, Jean, and Maurice Vaïsse. *Diplomatie et Outil Militaire: politique étrangère de la France, 1871–1969*. Paris: Imprimerie Nationale, 1987.

Duchêne, François. *Jean Monnet: The First Statesman of Interdependence*. New York: W. W. Norton, 1994.

Duroselle, Jean-Baptiste. *France and the United States: From the Beginnings to the Present*. Trans. Derek Coltman. Chicago: University of Chicago Press, 1978.

Eisenhower, Dwight D. *The Papers of Dwight David Eisenhower*, ed. Alfred D. Chandler, Jr. Baltimore, Md.: Johns Hopkins Press, 1970.

Elgey, Georgette. *Histoire de la IVe République*. Vol. I. *La République des illusions, 1945–1951*. Paris: Fayard, 1965.

Fontaine, André. *Histoire de la guerre froide*. Vol. I, *De la Révolution d'Octobre à la Guerre de Corée 1917–1950*. Paris: Fayard, 1965.

Furet, François. *Le passé d'une illusion: essai sur l'idée communiste au XXe siècle*. Paris: Robert Laffont/Calmann-Lévy, 1995.

Gaulle, Charles de. *The Complete War Memoirs of Charles de Gaulle*. 3 vols. Trans. Jonathan Griffin (vol. 1), Richard Howard (vols. 2 and 3). New York: Simon and Schuster, 1964.

———. *Discours et Messages*. 5 vols. Paris: Plon, 1970.

———. *The Edge of the Sword*. Trans. Gerard Hopkins. Westport, Conn.: Greenwood, 1960.

———. *Lettres, Notes et Carnets*. 12 vols. Paris: Plon, 1981.

———. *Memoirs of Hope: Renewal and Endeavor*. 2 vols. Trans. Terence Kilmartin. New York: Simon and Schuster, 1971.

Gerbet, Pierre. *La Construction de l'Europe*. Paris: Imprimerie Nationale, 1983.

———. *Le Relèvement, 1944–1949*. Paris: Imprimerie Nationale, 1991.

Gordon, Philip H. *A Certain Idea of France: French Security Policy and the Gaullist Legacy*. Princeton, N.J.: Princeton University Press, 1993.

Grémion, Pierre. *Intelligence de l'anticommunisme*. Paris: Fayard, 1995.

Grosser, Alfred. *Affaires extérieures: la politique de la France, 1944–1984*. Paris: Flammarion, 1989.

———. *The Western Alliance*. New York: Continuum, 1980.

Haftendorn, Helga. *NATO and the Nuclear Revolution: A Crisis of Credibility, 1966–1967*. Oxford: Clarendon Press, 1996.

Hoffmann, Stanley. *Decline or Renewal? France since the 1930s*. New York: Viking, 1974.

———. *In Search of France*. Cambridge, Mass.: Harvard University Press, 1963.

Ireland, Timothy P. *Creating the Entangling Alliance: The Origins of the North Atlantic Treaty Organization*. Westport, Conn.: Greenwood, 1981.

Juin, Alphonse. *Mémoires*. Vol. II. Paris: Arthème Fayard, 1960.

Kaplan, Lawrence S. *NATO and the United States: The Enduring Alliance*. Boston: Twayne, 1988.

Kaspi, André. *La libération de la France, Juin 1944–Janvier 1946*. Paris: Perrin, 1995.

Keylor, William R. *The Twentieth Century World: An International History*. New York: Oxford University Press, 1996.

Kissinger, Henry A. *Diplomacy*. New York: Simon and Schuster, 1994.

———. *The Troubled Partnership: A Reappraisal of the Atlantic Alliance*. New York: McGraw-Hill, 1965.

———. *Years of Upheaval*. Boston: Little, Brown, 1982.

Lacouture, Jean. *De Gaulle*. 2 vols. Trans. Alan Sheridan. New York: Simon and Schuster, 1991, 1992.

———. *De Gaulle*. 3 vols. Paris: Seuil, 1984, 1985, 1986.

———. *Léon Blum*. Paris: Seuil, 1977.

———. *Pierre Mendès France*. Paris: Seuil, 1981.

Laloy, Jean. *Yalta: Yesterday, Today, Tomorrow*. Trans. William R. Tyler. New York: Harper and Row, 1988.

Langer, William L., ed. *An Encyclopedia of World History*. Boston: Houghton Mifflin, 1972.

———. *Our Vichy Gamble*. New York: Knopf, 1947.

Lattre, Jean de. *Ne pas subir: écrits, 1914–1952*. Paris: Plon, 1984.

Maillard, Pierre. *De Gaulle et l'Allemagne: le rêve inachevé*. Paris: Plon, 1990.

Massigli, René. *Une comédie des erreurs*. Paris: Plon, 1978.

May, Ernest R., ed. *American Cold War Strategy: Interpreting NSC 68*. Boston: Bedford Books of St. Martin's Press, 1993.

McGeehan, Robert. *The German Rearmament Question*. Urbana: University of Illinois Press, 1971.

Mélandri, Pierre. *Les États-Unis face à l'unification de l'Europe, 1945–1954*. Paris: Pedone, 1980.

Mischlich, Robert. *Une mission secrète à Bonn*. Lausanne, Switzerland: Fondation Jean Monnet pour l'Europe et Centre de recherches européennes, 1986.

Mitterrand, François. *De l'Allemagne, de la France*. Paris: Odile Jacob, 1996.

———. *Mémoires Interrompus*. Paris: Odile Jacob, 1996.

Monnet, Jean. *Memoirs*. Garden City, N.Y.: Doubleday, 1978.

Murphy, Robert D. *Diplomat among Warriors*. Garden City, N.Y.: Doubleday, 1964.

Paxton, Robert O., and Nicholas Wahl, eds. *De Gaulle and the United States: A Centennial Reappraisal*. Providence, R.I.: Berg, 1993.

Peyrefitte, Alain. *C'était de Gaulle*. Paris: Fayard, 1994.

Rearden, Steven L. *History of the Office of the Secretary of Defense*. Vol. I, *The Formative Years, 1947–1950*. Washington, D.C.: Historical Office, Office of the Secretary of Defense, 1984.

Rouanet, Pierre. *Mendès France au pouvoir, 1954–1955*. Paris: Robert Laffont, 1965.

Schnabel, James F. *The History of the Joint Chiefs of Staff: The Joint Chiefs of Staff and National Policy*. Vol. I, 1945–1947. Wilmington, Del.: Michael Glazier, 1979.

Schuman, Robert. *French Policy Toward Germany since the War*. London: Oxford University Press, 1954.

Spaak, Paul-Henri. *Combats Inachevés*. Vol. I: de *l'Indépendance à l'Alliance*. Paris: Fayard, 1969.

Steel, Ronald. *Walter Lippmann and the American Century*. Boston: Little, Brown, 1980.

Teitgen, Pierre-Henri. *Faites entret le témoin suivant, 1940–1958, de la Résistance à la Cinquième République*. Paris: Ouest-France, 1988.

Truman, Harry S. *Memoirs*. Vol. I, *Year of Decisions*. Garden City: Doubleday, 1956.

———. *Memoirs*. Vol. II, *Years of Trial and Hope*. Garden City: Doubleday, 1956.

Vaïsse, Maurice. *Les relations internationales depuis 1945*. Paris: Armand Colin, 1990.

Vaïsse, Maurice, Pierre Mélandri, and Frédéric Bozo, eds. *La France et l'OTAN, 1949–1996*. Brussels: Éditions Complexe, 1996.

Wall, Irwin M. *The United States and the Making of Postwar France, 1945–54*. Cambridge: Cambridge University Press, 1991.

Young, John W. *France, the Cold War and the Western Alliance*. Leicester, U.K.: Leicester University Press, 1990.

ARTICLES

Bozo, Frédéric, and Jérôme Paolini. "Trois Allemagnes, deux Europes et la France." *Politique Étrangère* 1 (1990): 119.

Buchan, Alastair. "The Multilateral Force: An Historical Perspective." *Adelphi Papers* No. 13. London: The Institute for Strategic Studies, October 1964.

DePorte, Anton W. "De Gaulle's Europe: Playing the Russian Card." *French Politics and Society* 8 No. 4 (fall 1990): 26.

Duval, Marcel. "Élaboration et developpement du concept français de dissuasion." *Relations internationales* no. 59 (autumn 1989): 371.

Hoffmann, Stanley. "The Man Who Would be France." *The New Republic*, 17 December 1990, 29.

Jouve, Edmond, and Maurice Couve de Murville. "Mémorandum de 1958 sur l'O.T.A.N.'s." *Espoir* no. 15 (June 1976): 2.

Katz, Milton. "The Marshall Plan After Twenty Years." *The Foreign Service Journal* (June 1967): 1.

Rouche, Geneviève. "Le Quai d'Orsay face au problème de la souveraineté Allemande." *Revue d'Histoire Diplomatique* no. 104 (1990): 38.

Soutou, Georges-Henri. "The French Military Program for Nuclear Energy, 1945–1981." *Nuclear History Program Occasional Paper 3* (College Park, Md., Center for International Security Studies, University of Maryland, 1989).

Yost, David S. "France and Conventional Defense in Central Europe." *European American Institute for Security Research Paper Number 7*, spring 1984.

PARTS OF COLLECTED WORKS

De Gaulle et la Nation face aux problèmes de défense (1945–1946), colloquium organized by the Institut d'Histoire du Temps Présent and the Institut

Charles-de-Gaulle, October 21–22, 1982, Collection Espoir, Paris, Plon, 1983.

Gaddis, John Lewis. "The United States and the Question of a Sphere of Influence in Europe, 1945–1949. In *Western Security: The Formative Years. European and Atlantic Defense, 1947–1953*, ed. Olav Riste. New York: Columbia University Press, 1985.

Hoffmann, Stanley. "The Foreign Policy of Charles de Gaulle." In *The Diplomats 1939–1979*, ed. Gordon A. Craig and Francis L. Loewenheim. Princeton, NJ: Princeton University Press, 1994.

———. "The Nation, Nationalisms and After: The Case of France." In *The Tanner Lectures on Human Values*, Vol. 15. ed. Grethe B. Peterson. Salt Lake City: University of Utah Press, 1994.

L'Aventure de la bombe: De Gaulle et la dissuasion nucléaire (1958–1969), colloquium organized by the University of Franche Comté and the Institut Charles-de-Gaulle, September 27–29, 1984. Paris: Plon, Collection Espoir, 1985.

Vaïsse, Maurice. "L'Échec d'une Europe franco-britannique ou comment le pacte de Bruxelles fut créé et délaissé." In *Les Débuts de la construction européenne*, ed. Raymond Poidevin. Brussels: Bruylant, 1986, 369.

DOCUMENTATION CONSULTED

France

Archives du Quai d'Orsay, Paris.
Service Historique de l'Armée de Terre, Château de Vincennes, Paris.

United States

National Archives II, College Park, Maryland.
Dwight D. Eisenhower Presidential Library, Abilene, Kansas.
Lyndon Baines Johnson Presidential Library, Austin, Texas.
John F. Kennedy Presidential Library, Boston, Massachusetts.
Harry S. Truman Presidential Library, Independence, Missouri.

Index

About the Author

CHARLES G. COGAN is an Associate of the Charles Warren Center for Studies in American History, and an Affiliate of the John M. Olin Institute for Strategic Studies and the Center for European Studies, Harvard University. He is the author of *Oldest Allies, Guarded Friends: The United States and France Since 1940* (Praeger, 1994) and *Charles de Gaulle: A Brief Biography with Documents* (1996). Cogan spent 37 years in the Central Intelligence Agency. From 1979 to 1984 he was chief of the Operations Directorate's Near East and South Asia Division. He was awarded the Distinguished Intelligence Medal in 1989. In the same year, he was assigned to the Intelligence and Policy Project at the John F. Kennedy School of Government and after leaving the CIA he earned a doctorate in public administration from Harvard in 1992. His published articles have dealt primarily with French-American relations, with the Middle East, and with intelligence and defense issues.